Monkeys Made of Sockies

A Sock Monkey Coloring Book
For The Fun At Heart

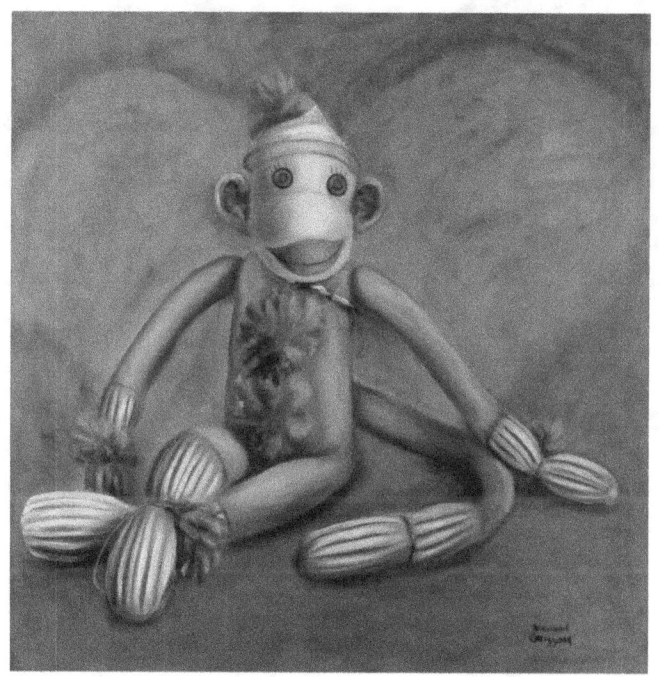

By Shannon A. Grissom

http://www.monkeymadeofsockies.com

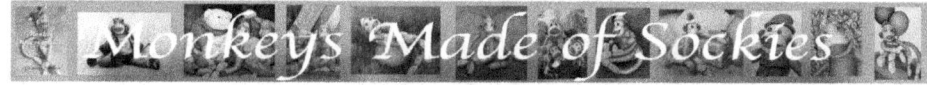
Table of Fun!

01	Life is Good	23	Golfer
02	Biker Dude	24	Mother and Child
03	Back	25	Mother's Day
04	Birthday	26	Night Night
05	Blur	27	Hear No Bad Stuff
06	Buddies	28	See No Bad Stuff
07	Christmas Tree	29	Speak No Bad Stuff
08	Dancer	30	Over The Top
09	Diva	31	Patricia
10	Easter	32	Pot-o-Gold
11	Face	33	Pretzel
12	Escape	34	Profile
13	Friends	35	Rhyme And Reason
14	Grad	36	Stocking
15	Halloween	37	Sweetheart
16	Head Over Heels	38	Touchdown
17	Heal	39	Uncle Frank
18	Hide And Seek	40	Valentine
19	Hugs	41	Victory
20	I Will Remember You	42	Wanna Be A Rock N Roll Star
21	Jump For Joy	43	Accordion
22	Kazoo		

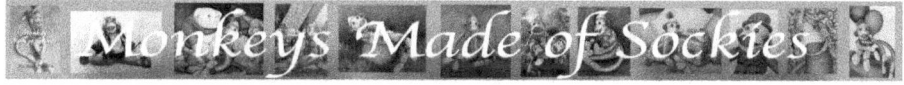

For Mom

Life Is Good

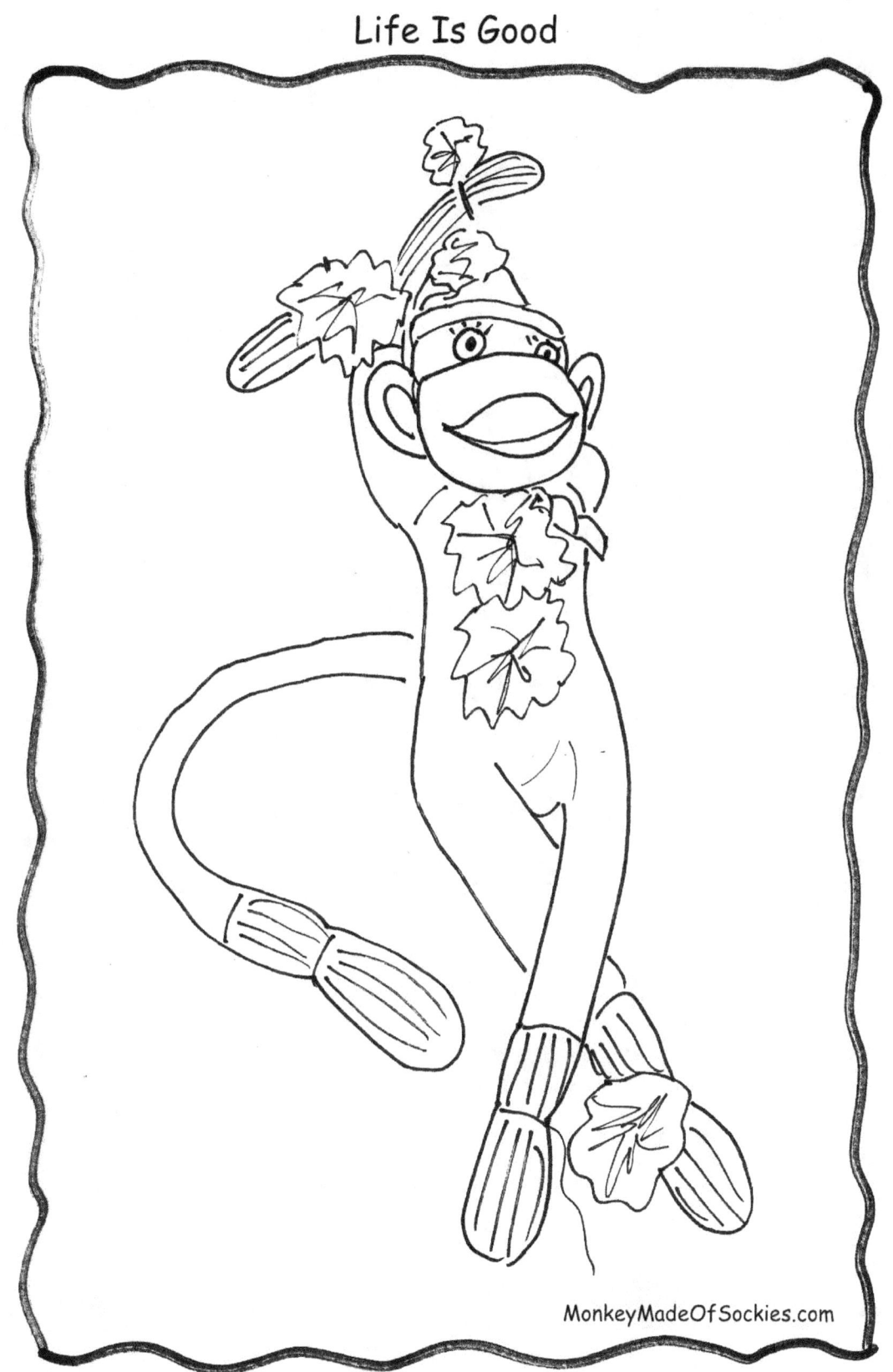

BIKER DUDE MADE OF SOCKIES

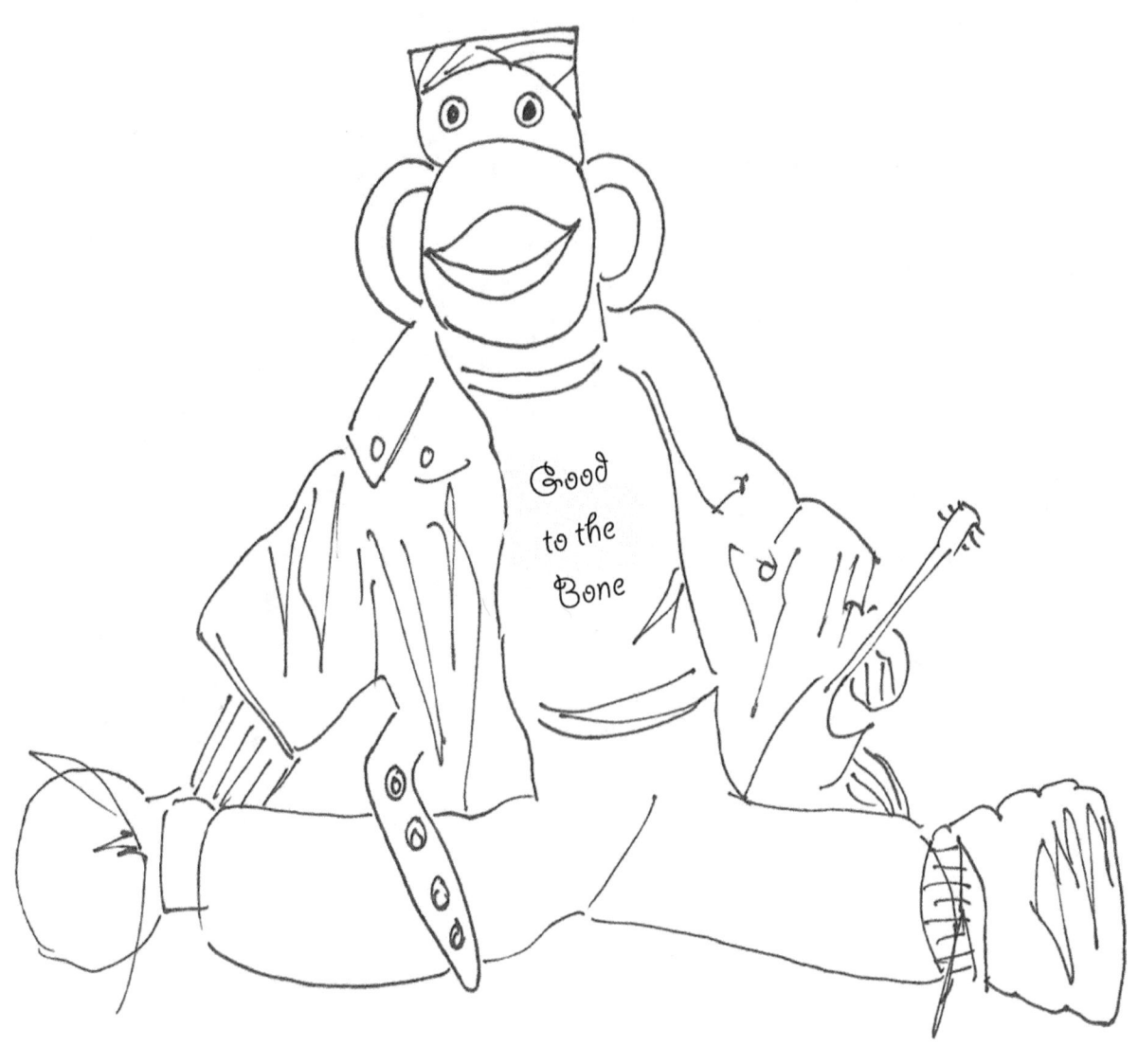

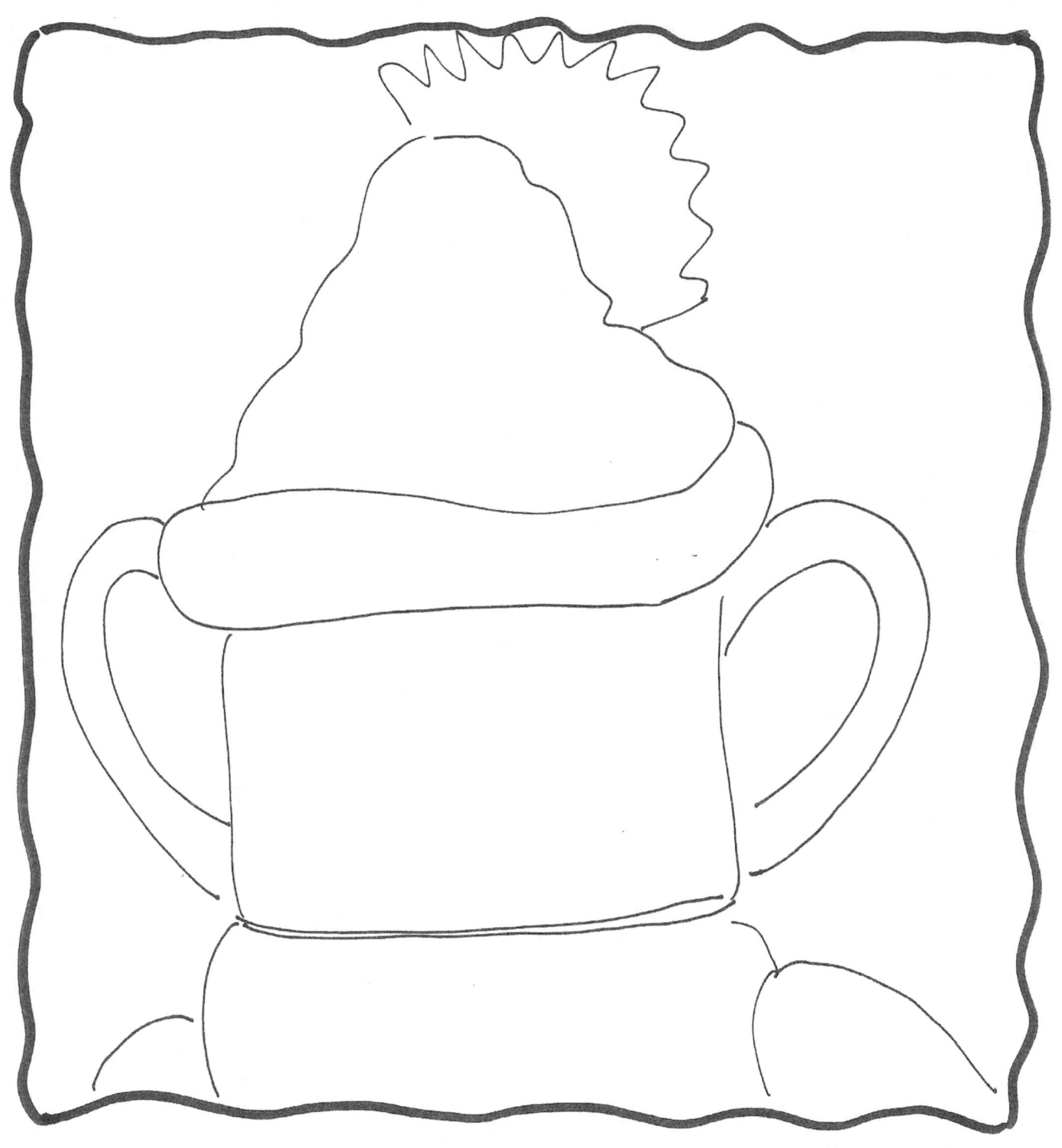

Monkey Made of Sockies Back

Birthday Made of Sockies

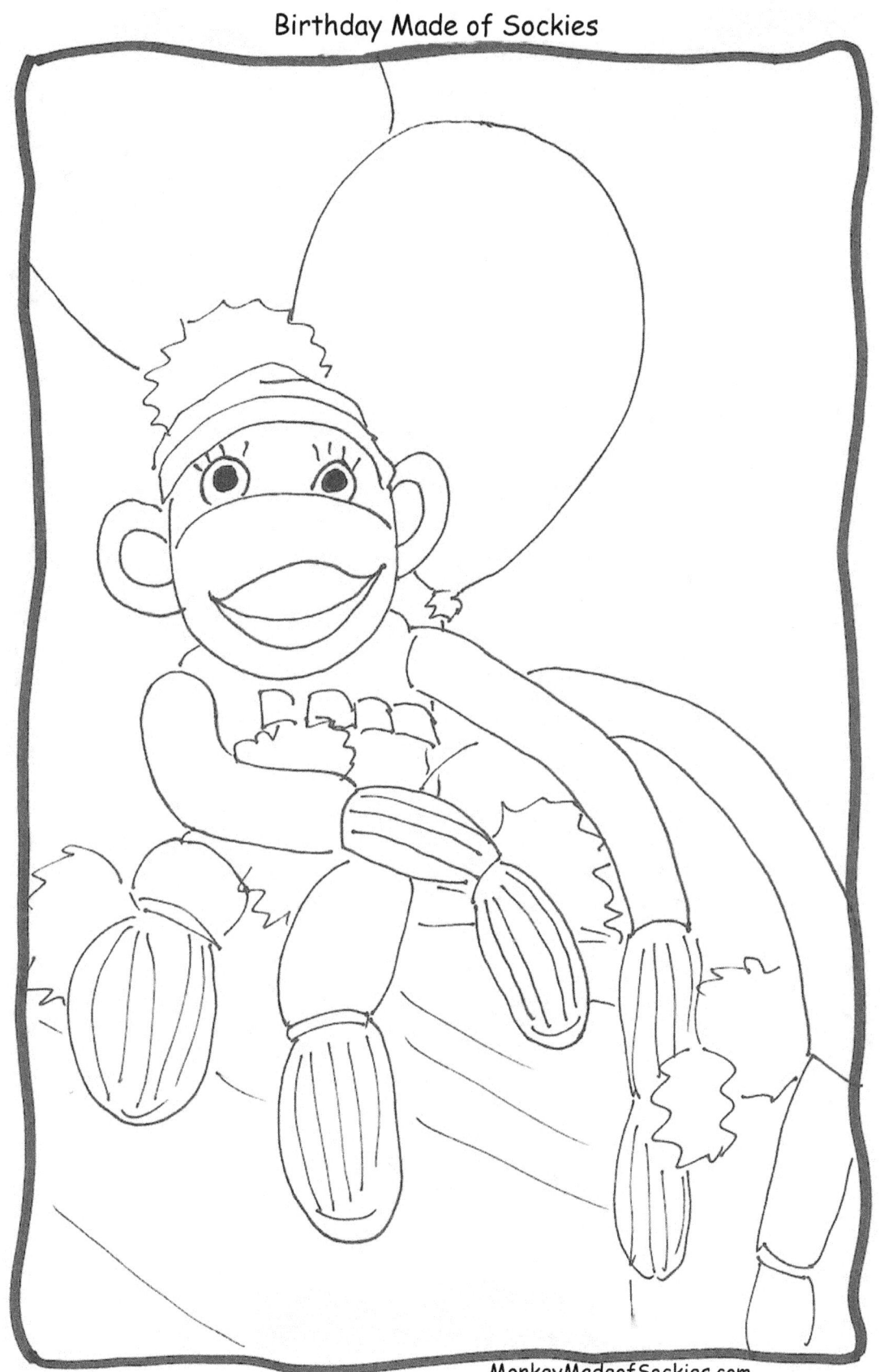

MonkeyMadeofSockies.com

Blur

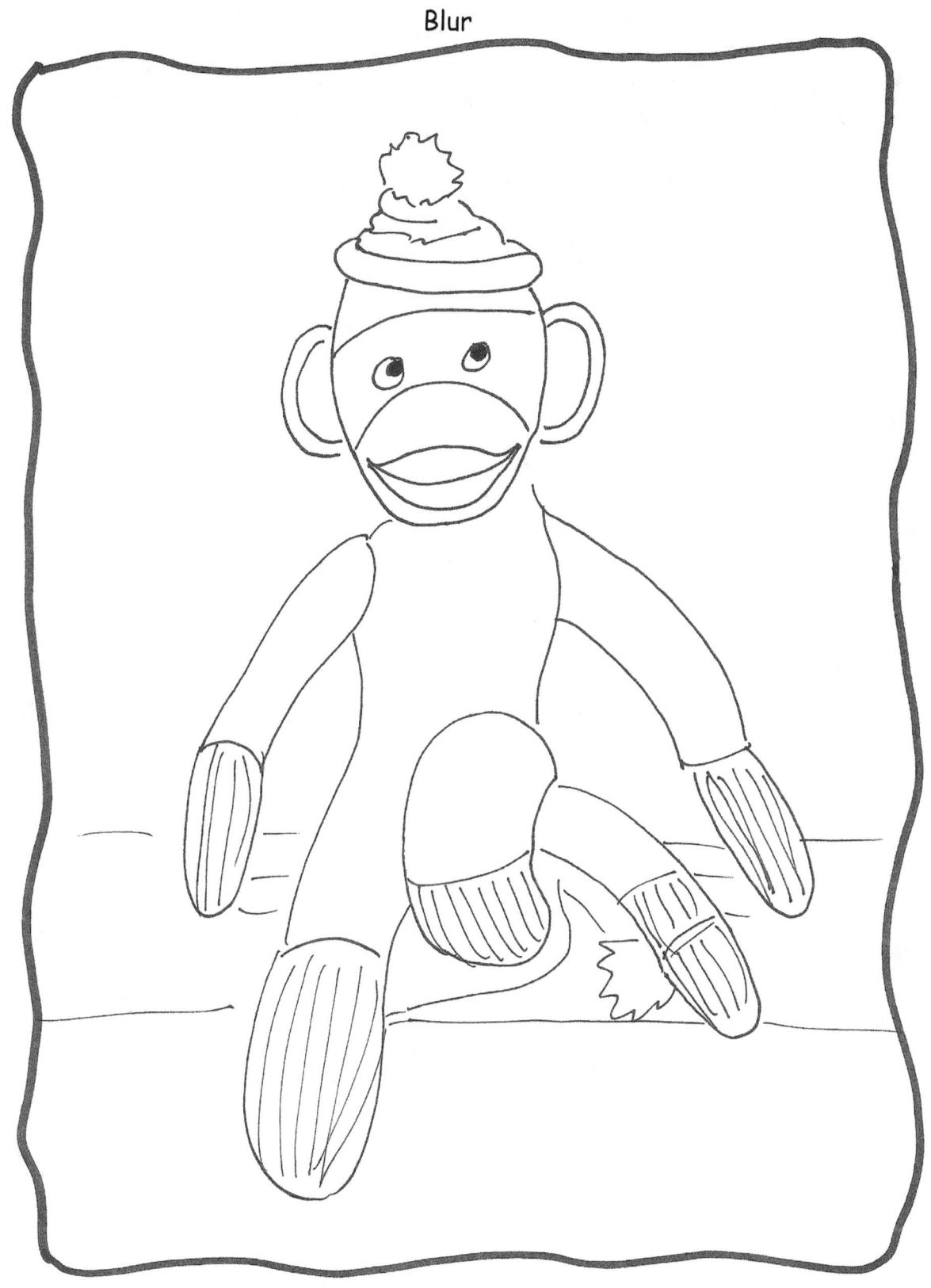

Buddies

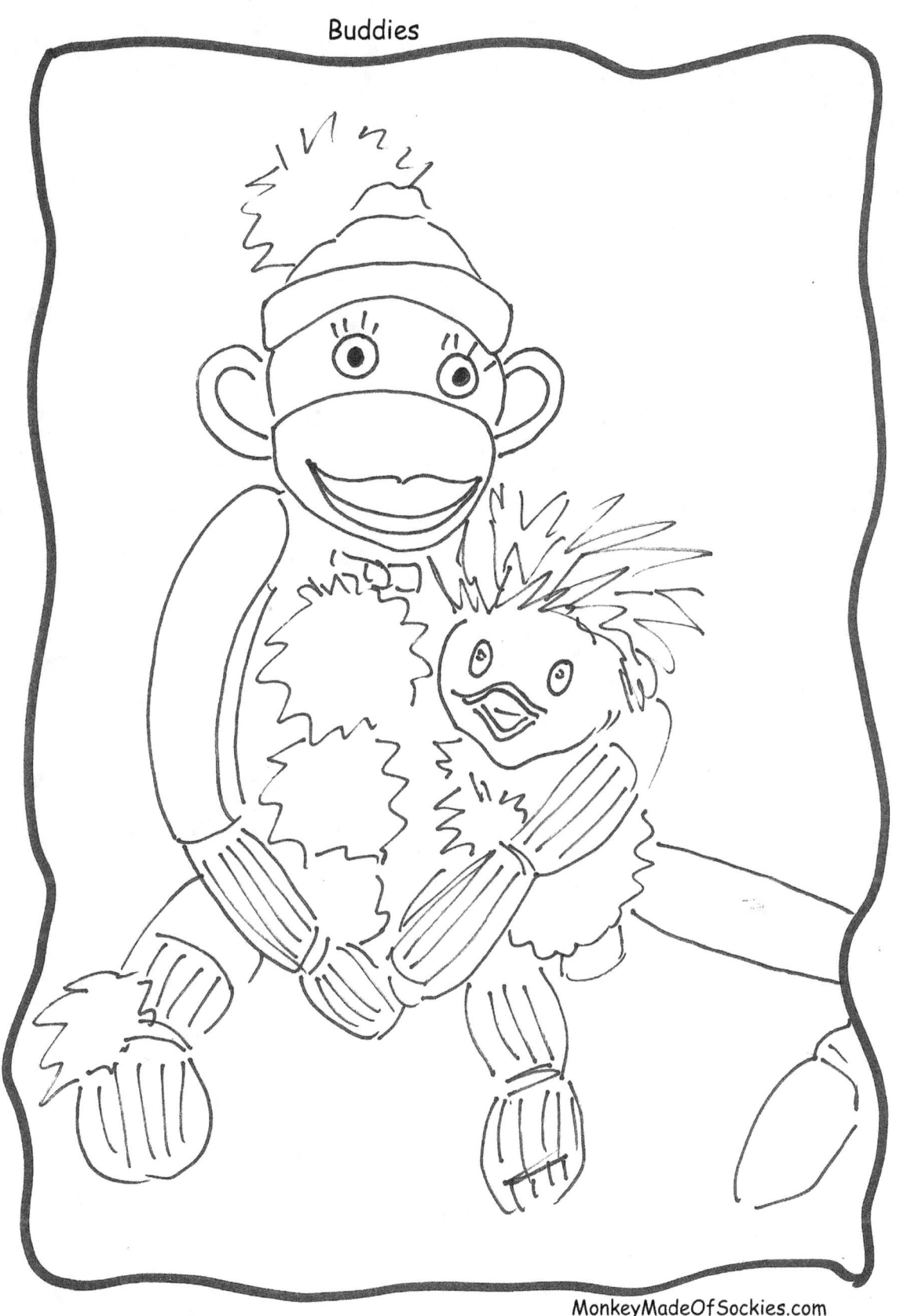

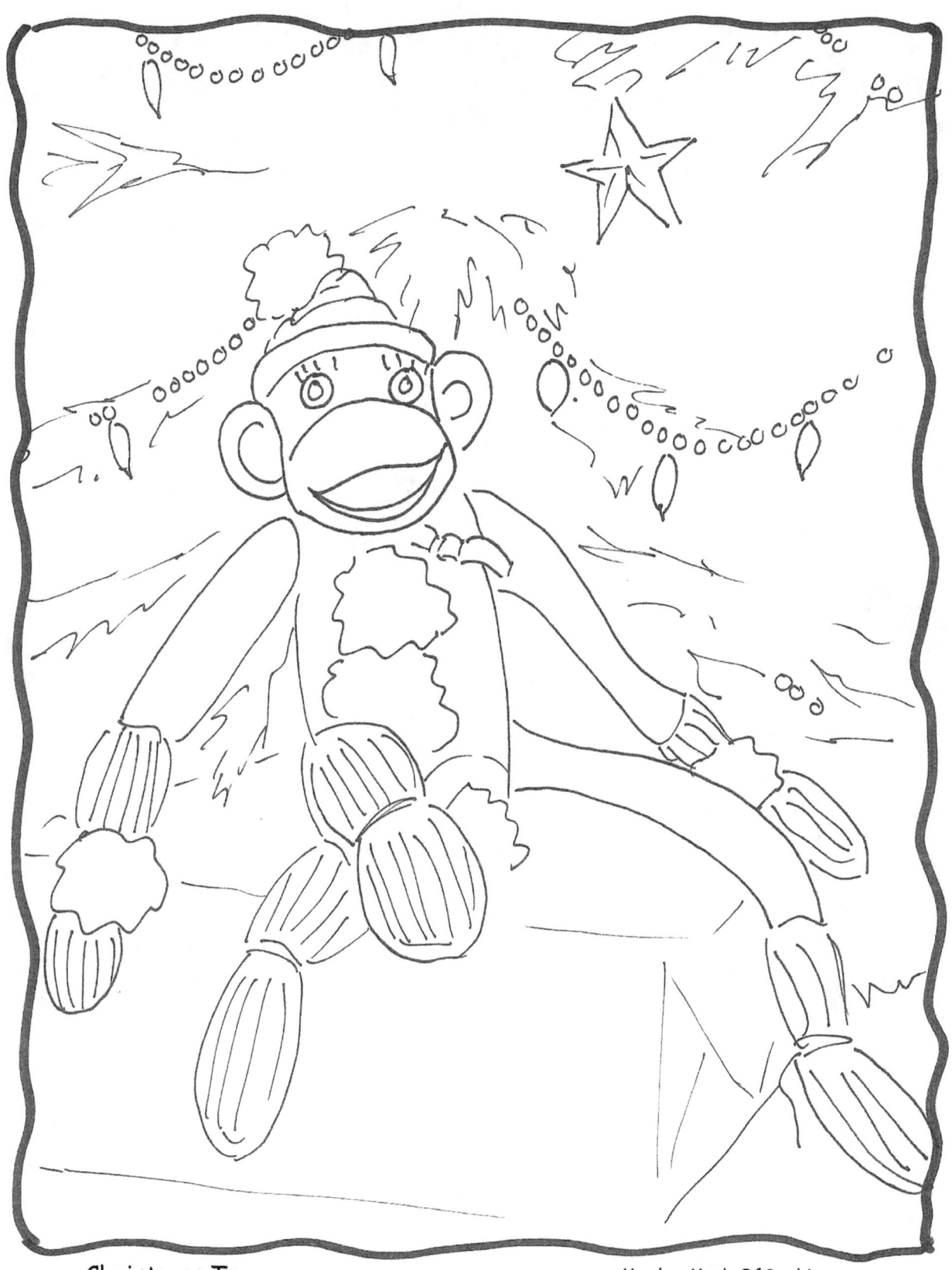

Christmas Tree

Dancer

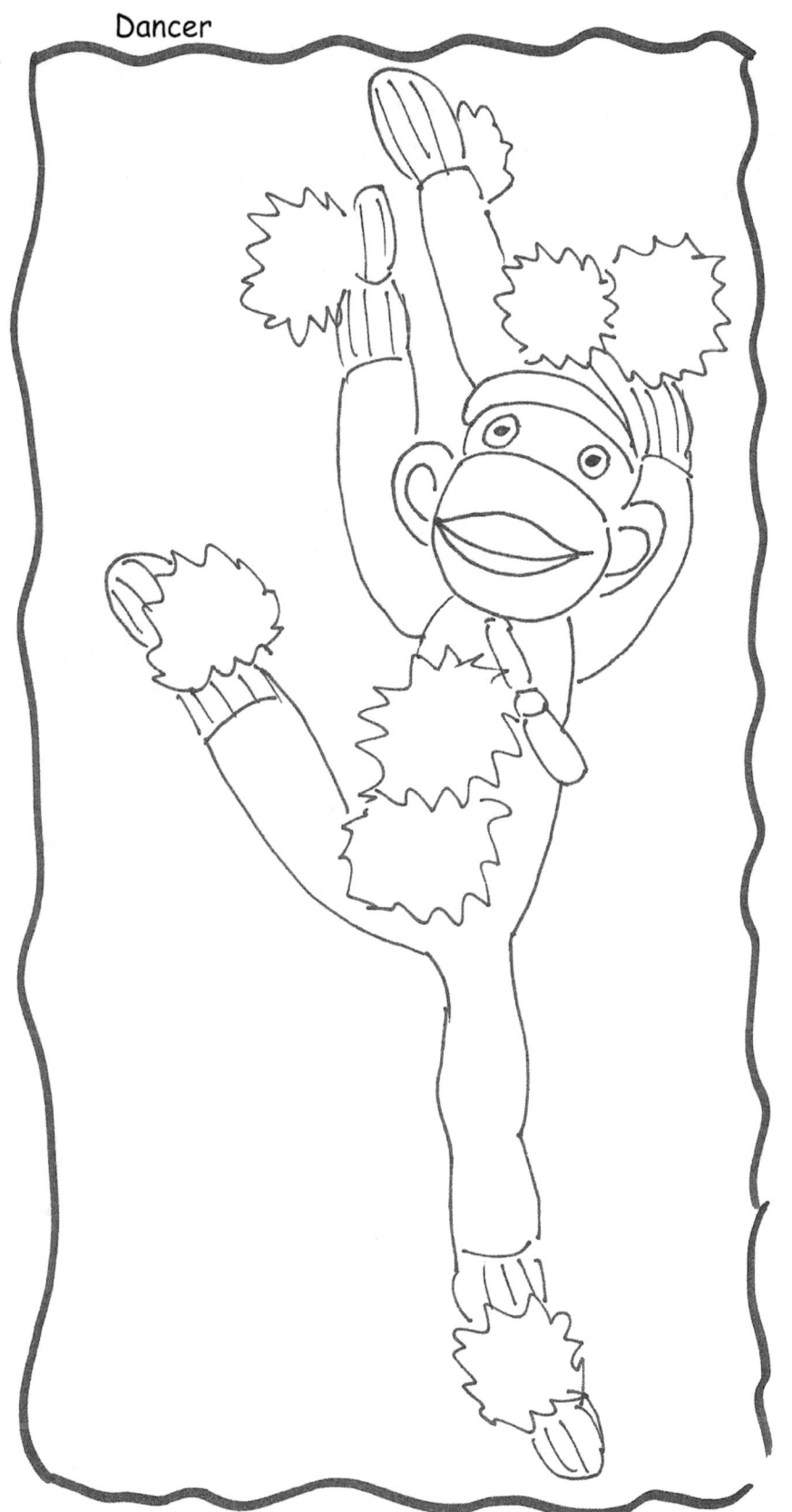

Diva

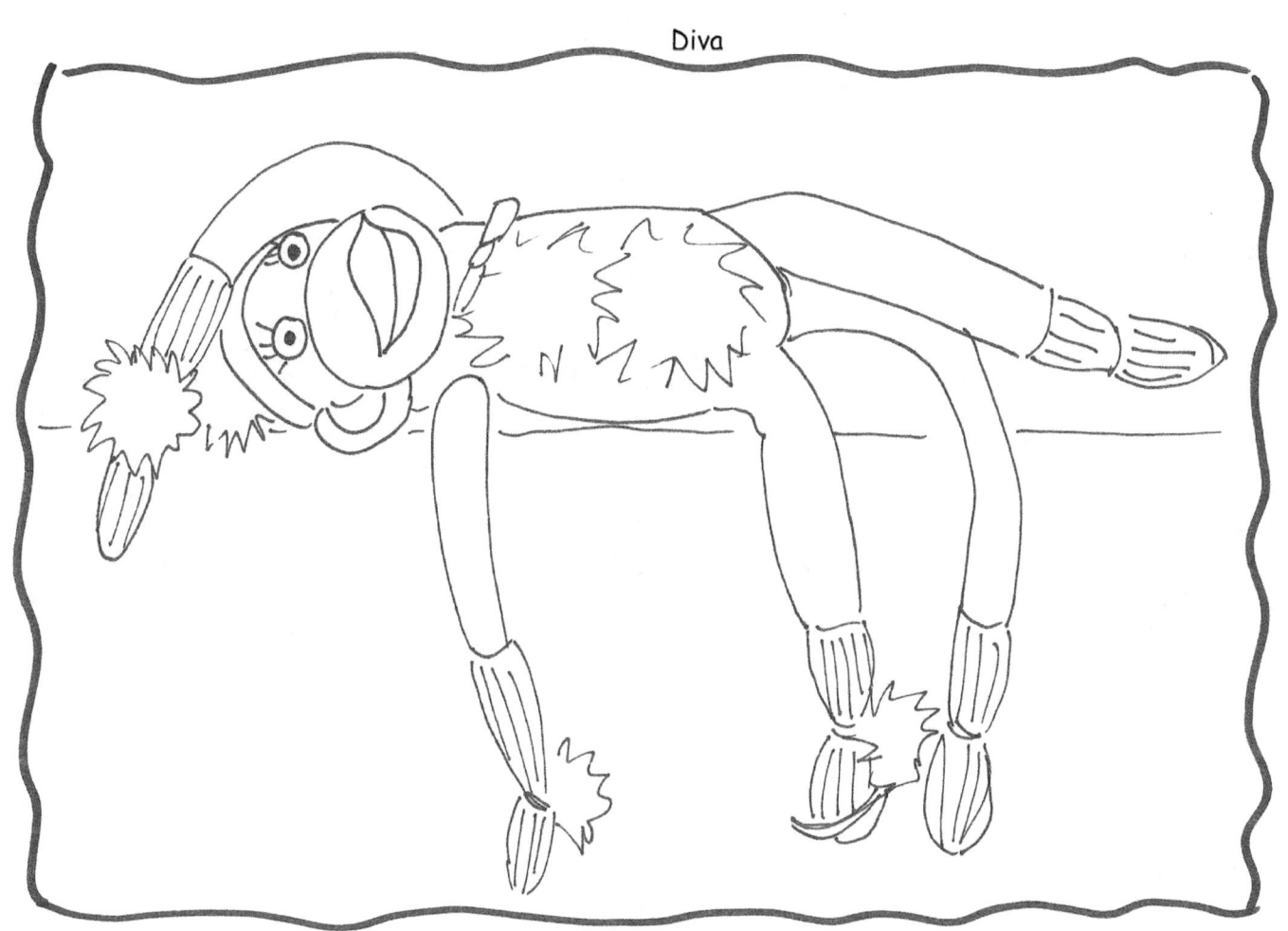

Easter

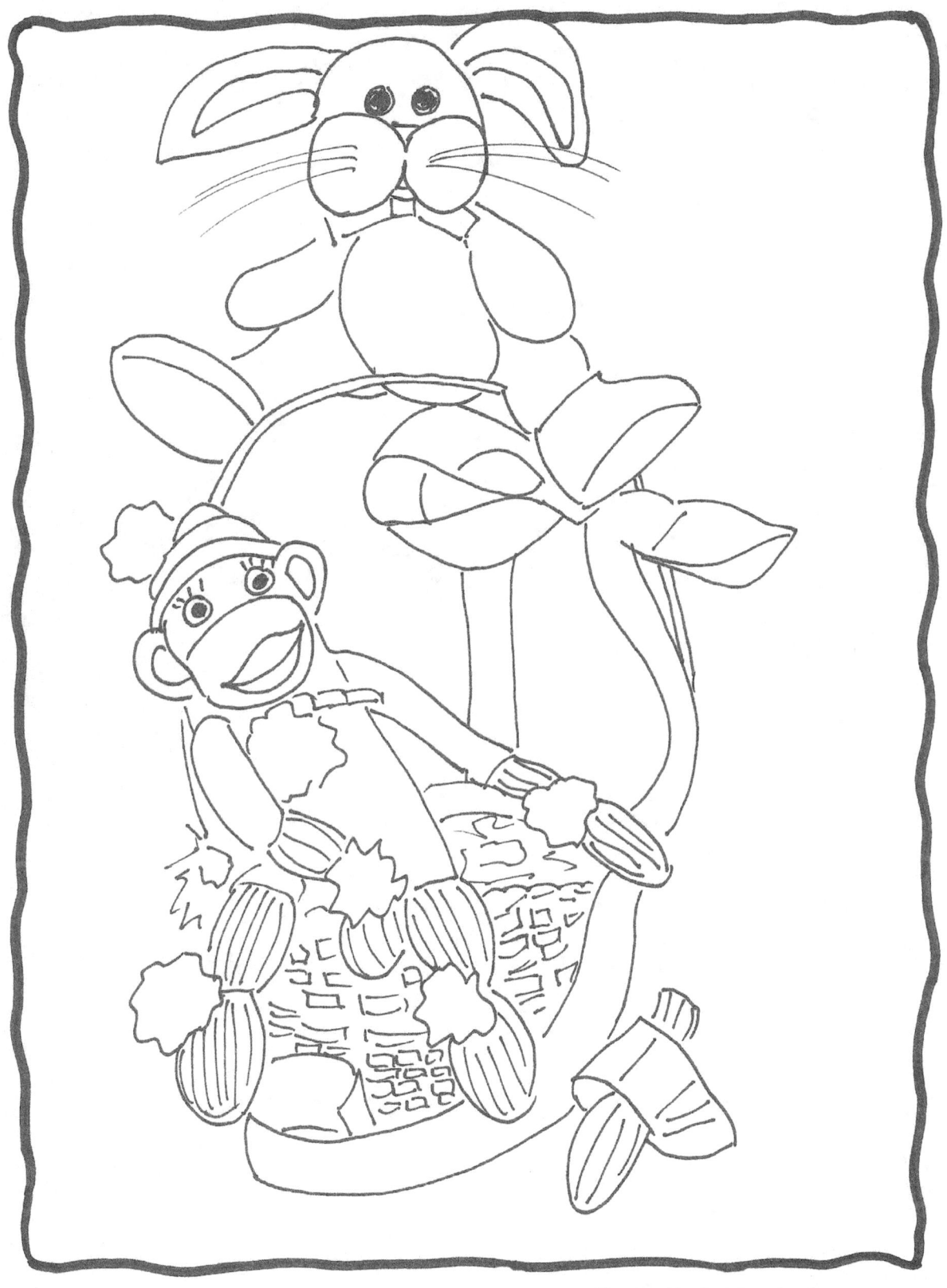

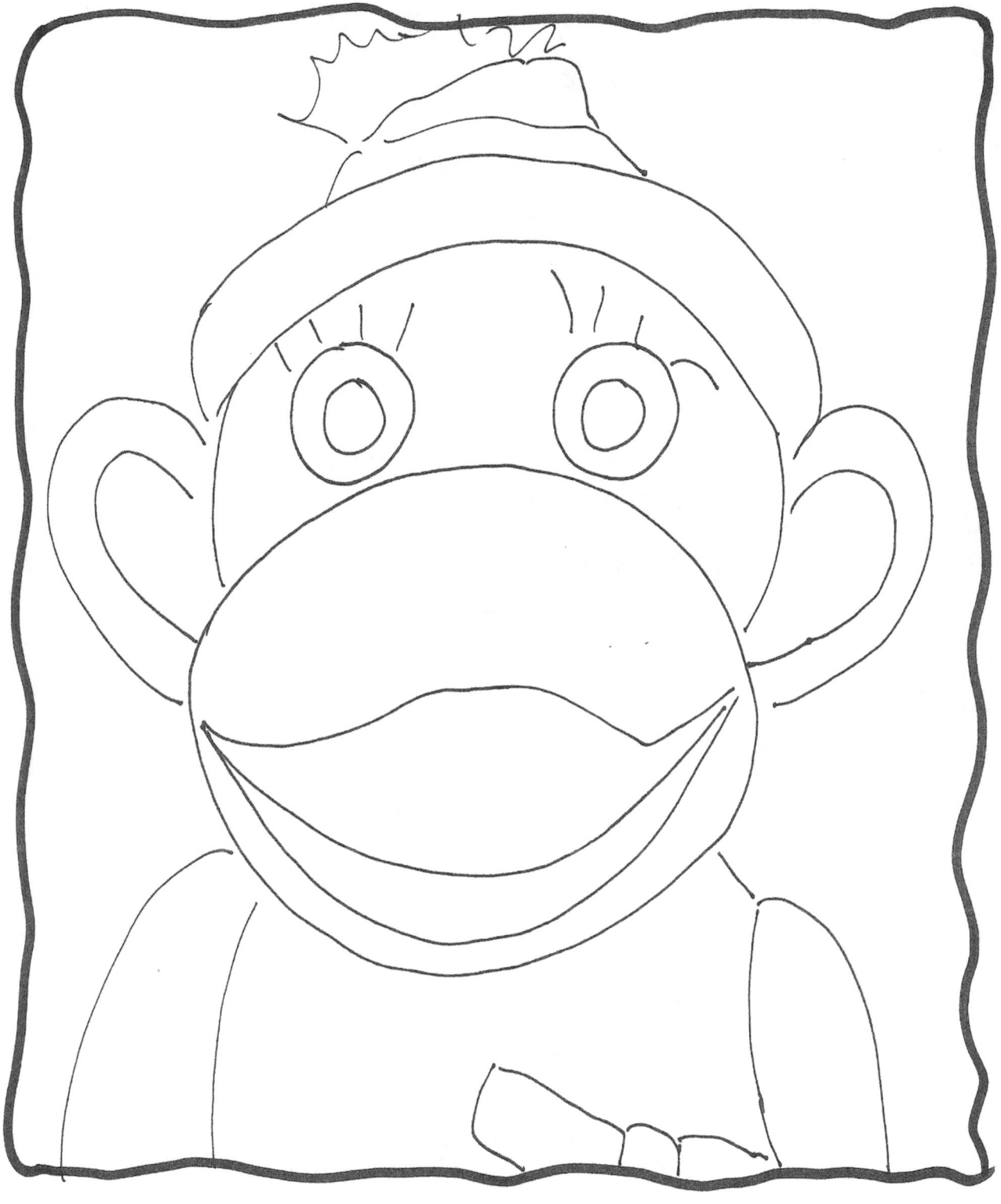

Face

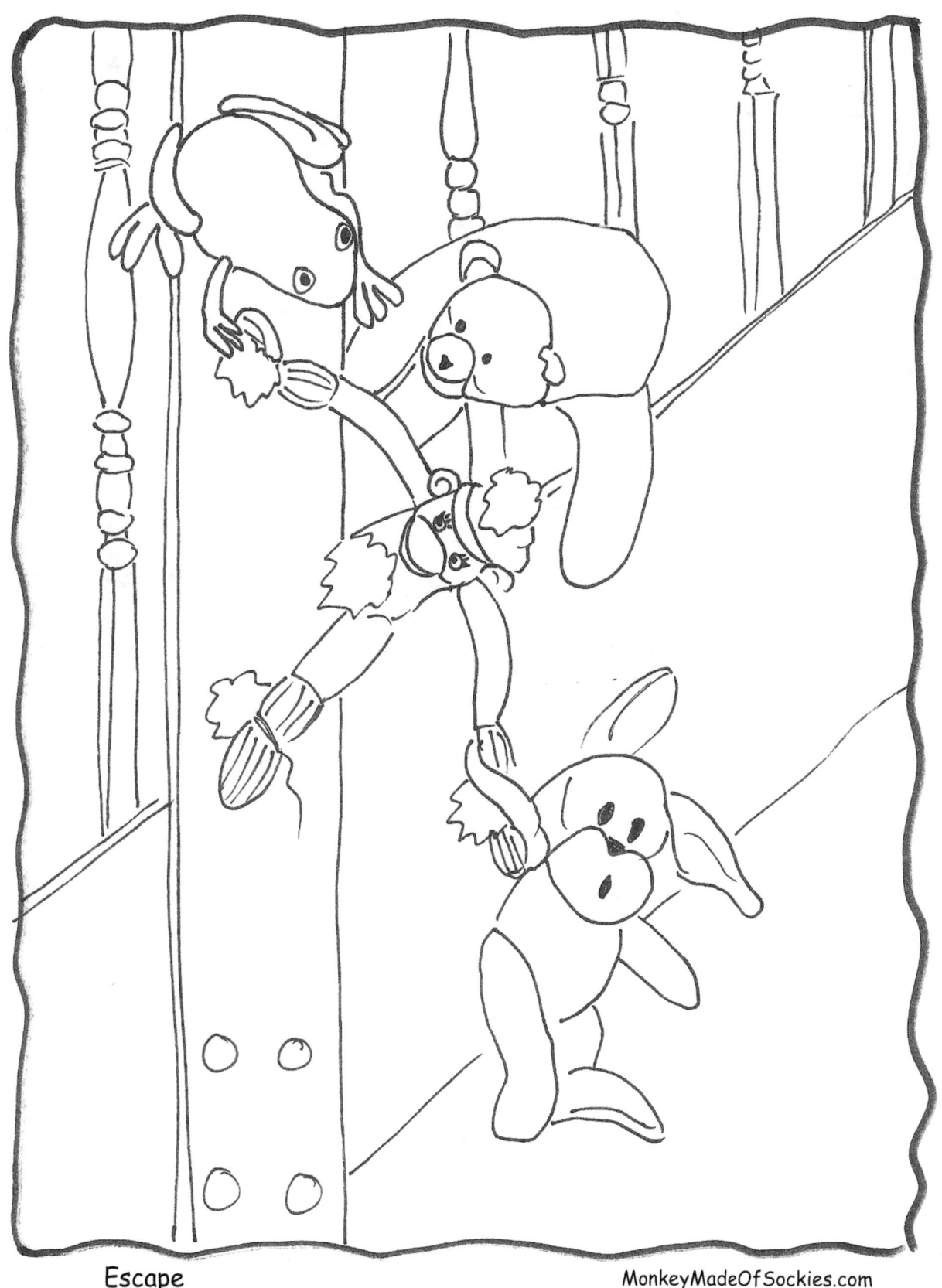

Escape

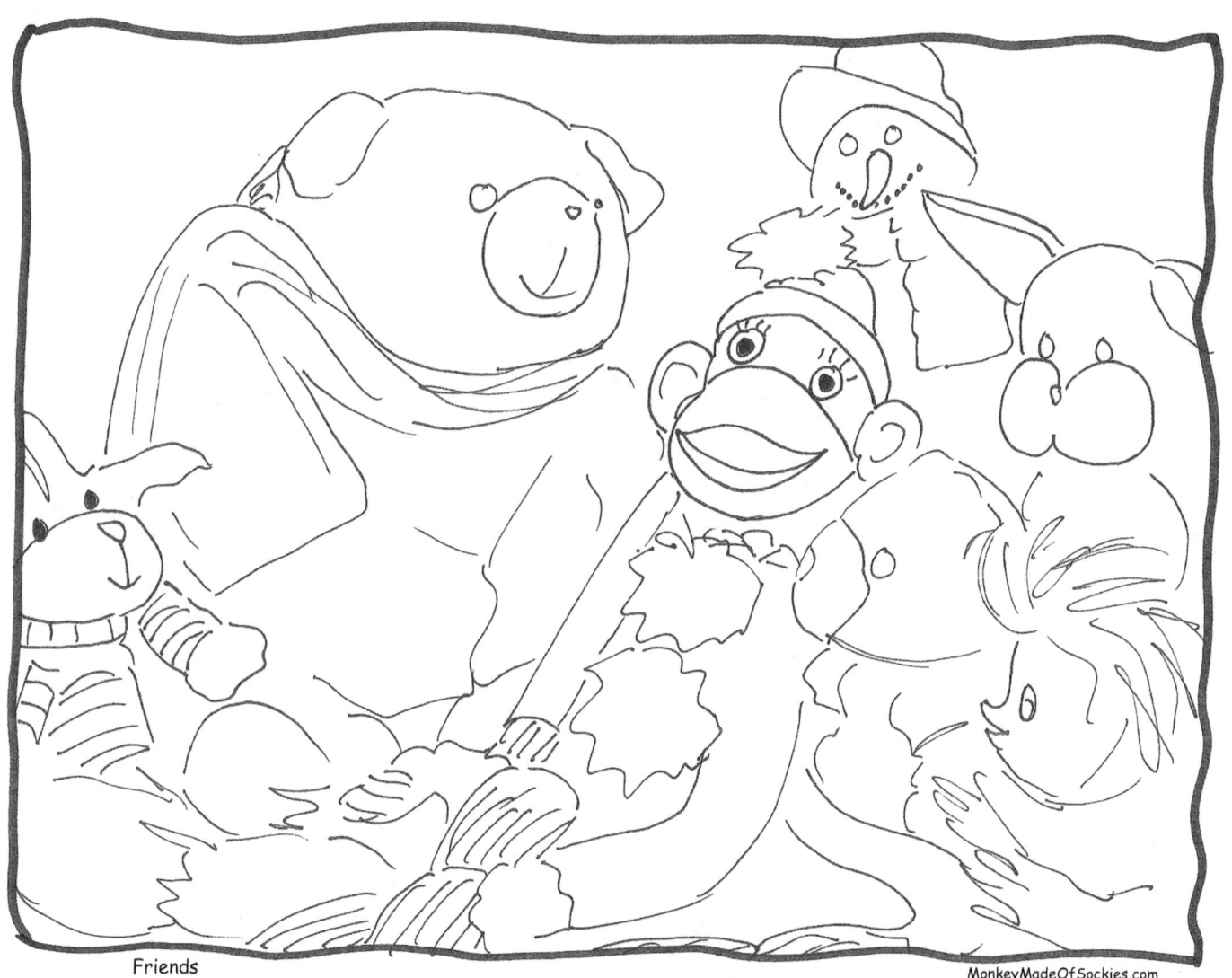

Friends

Grad

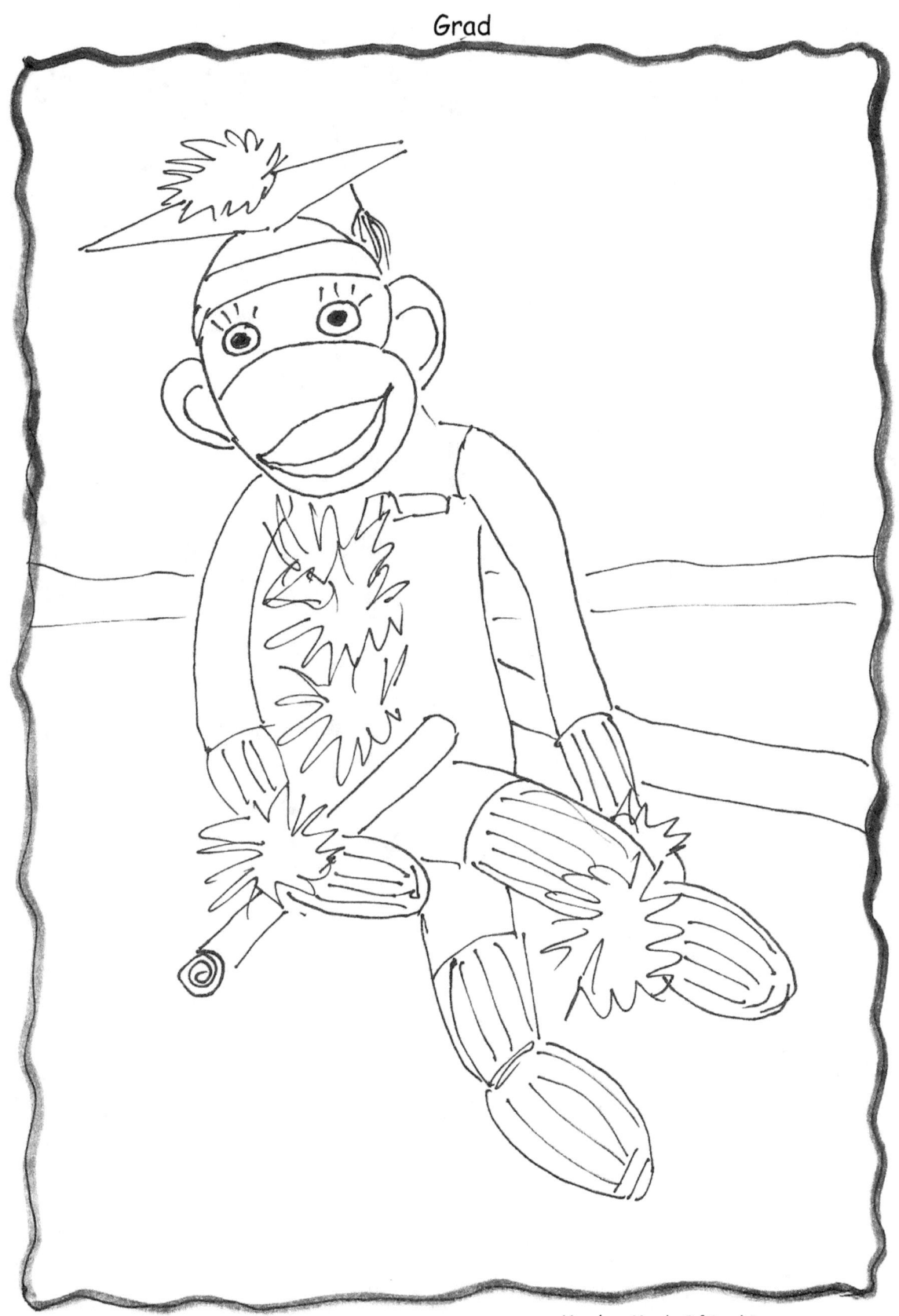

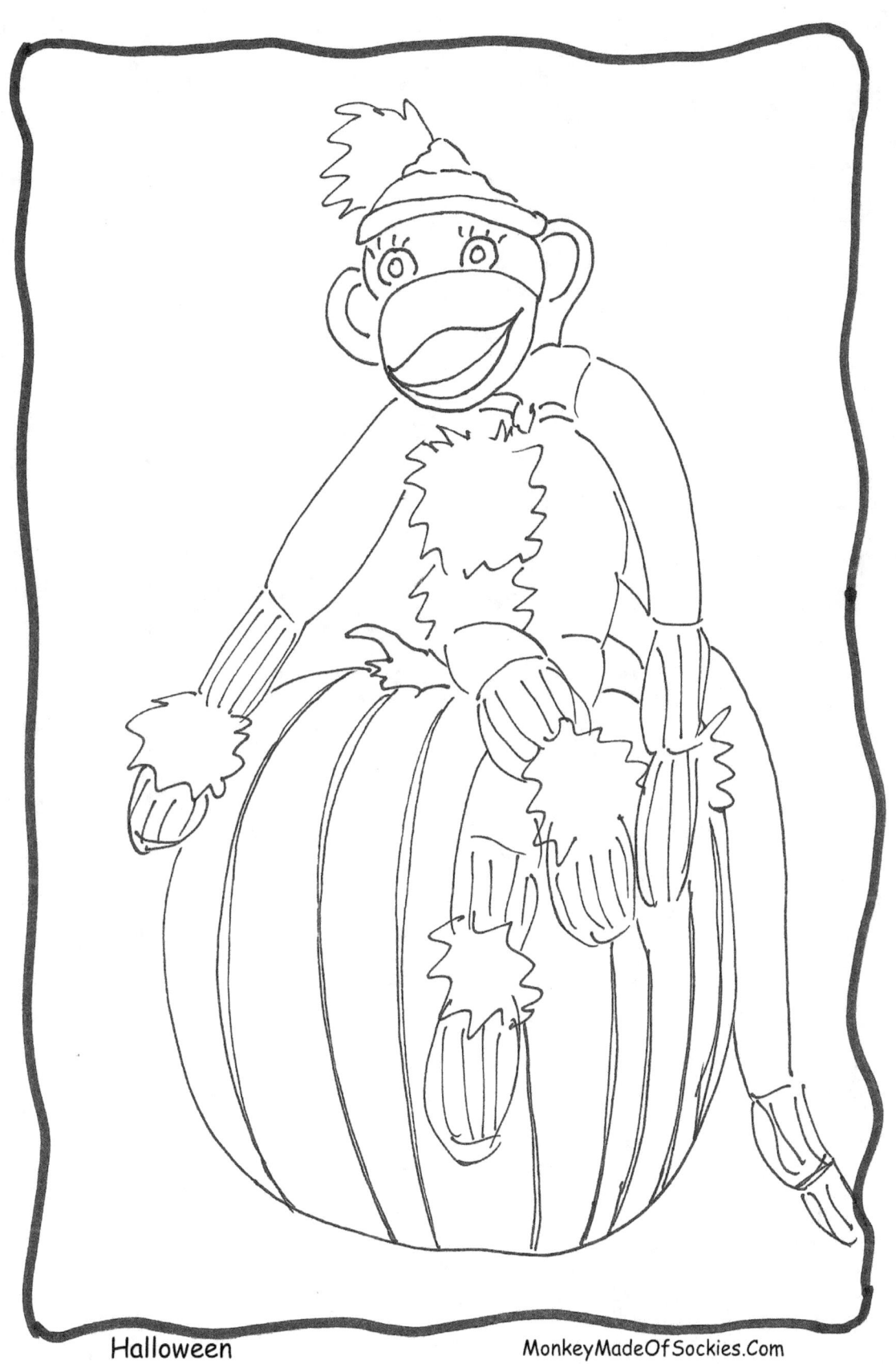

Halloween

Head Over Heels

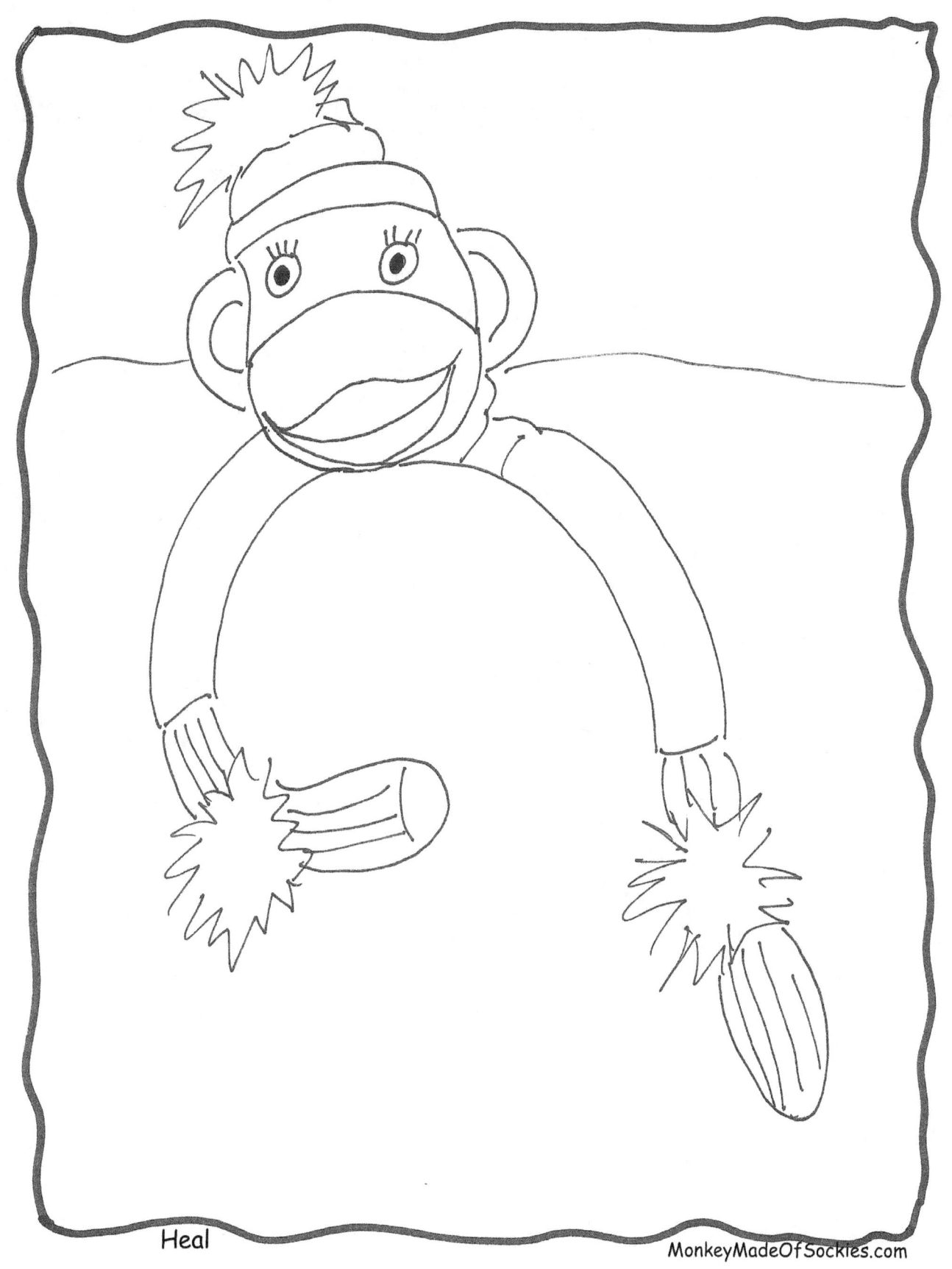

Heal

Hide And Seek

Hugs

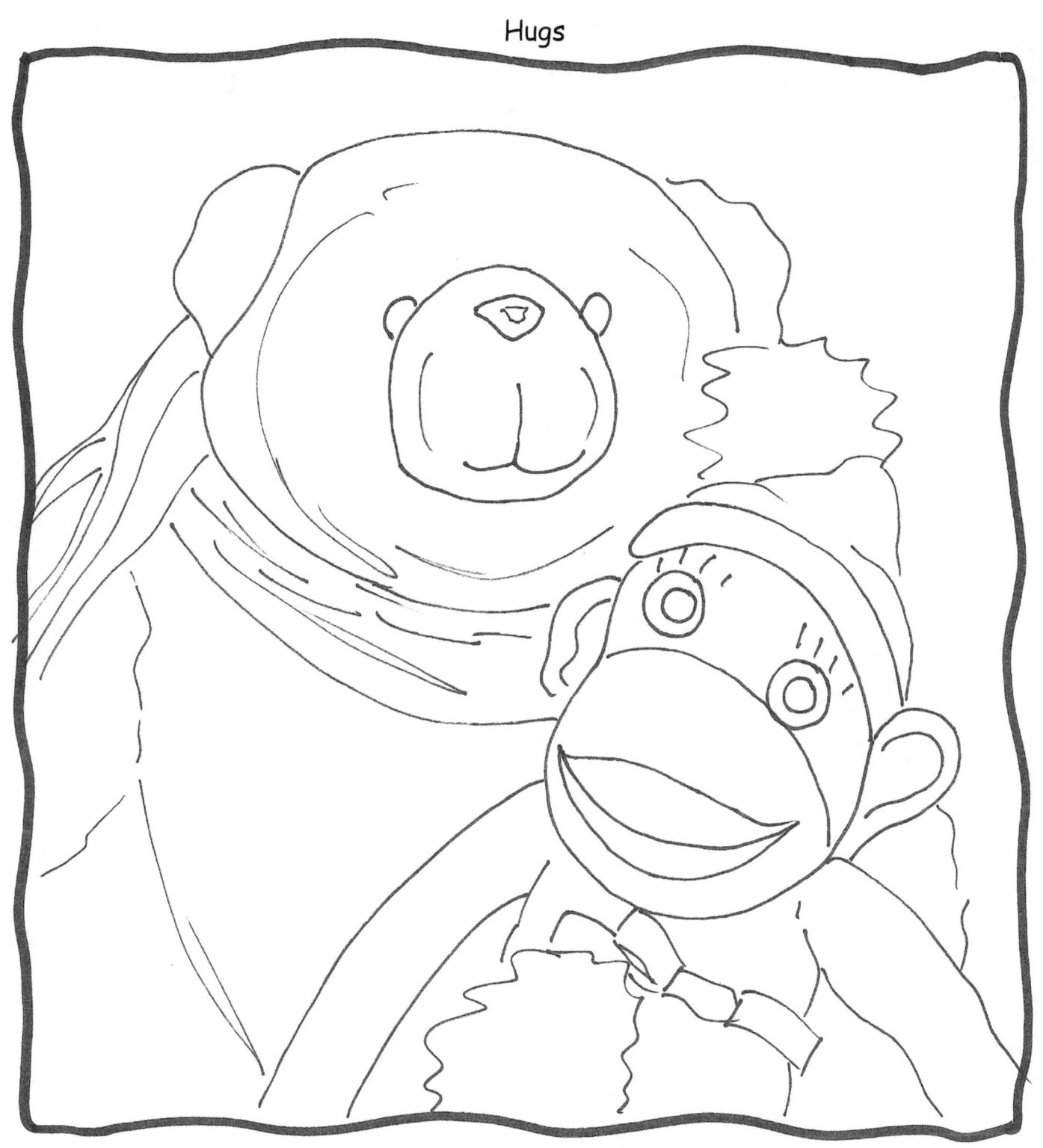

I Will Remember You

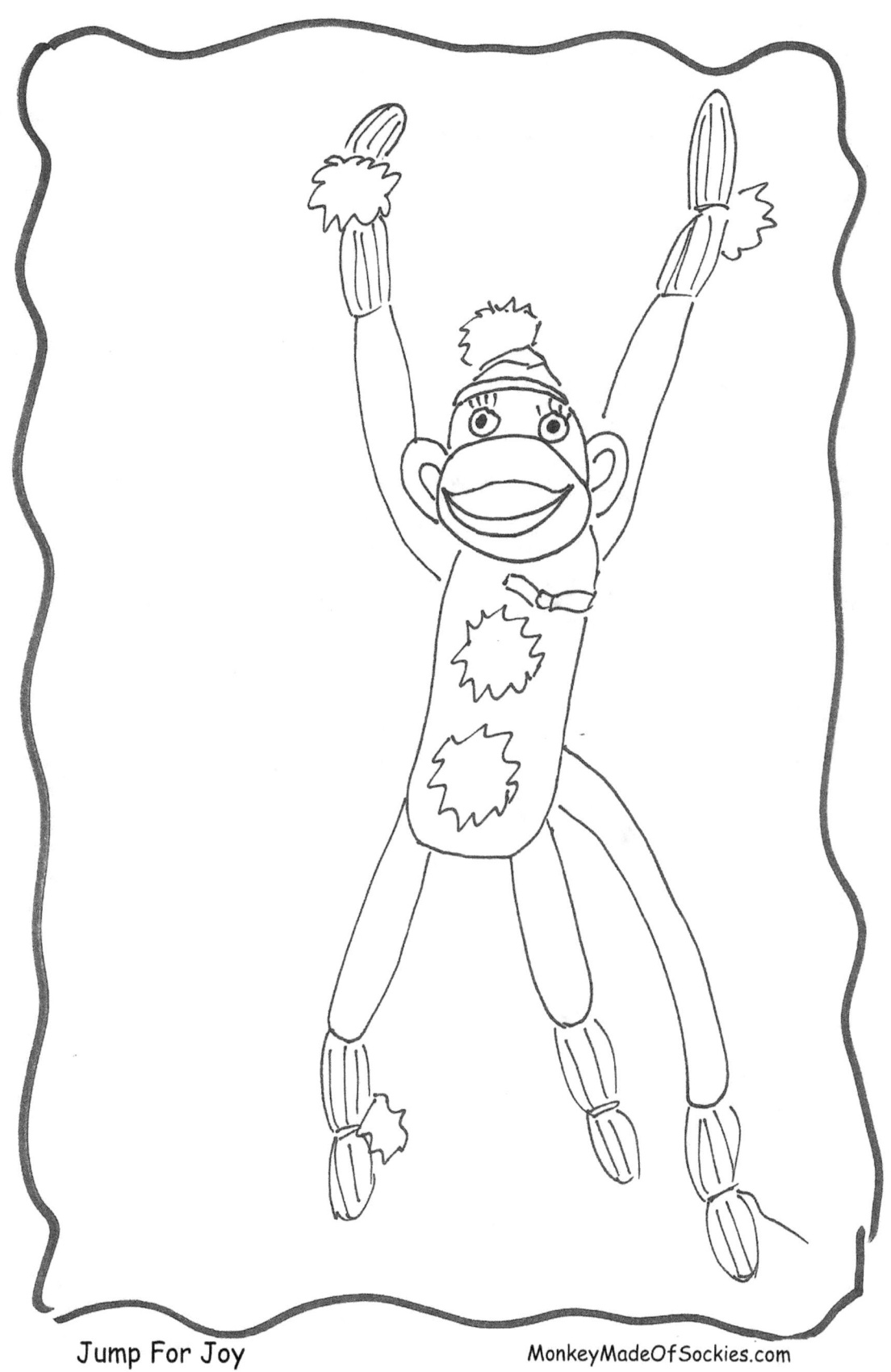

Jump For Joy

MonkeyMadeOfSockies.com

Kazoo

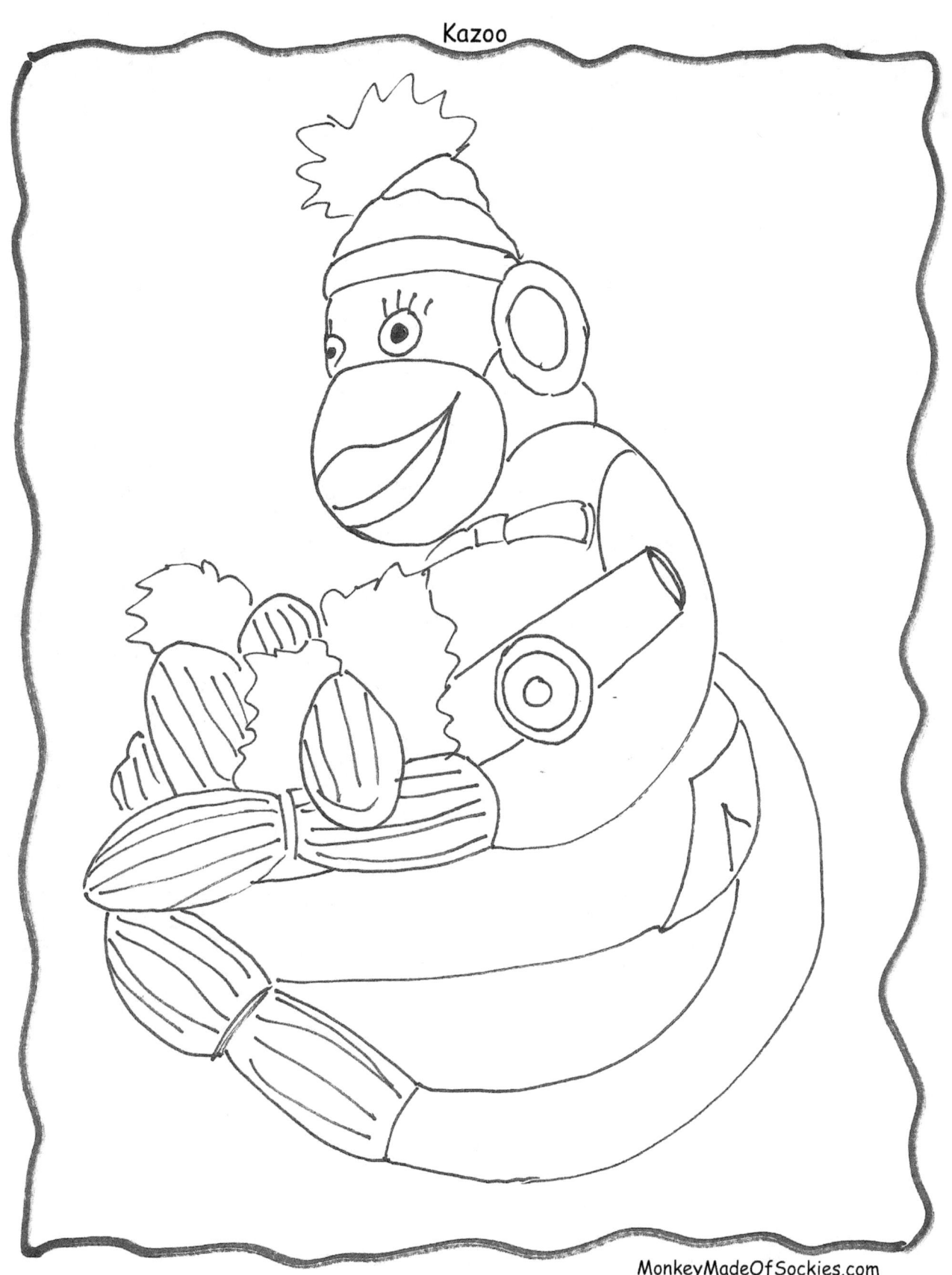

Golfer

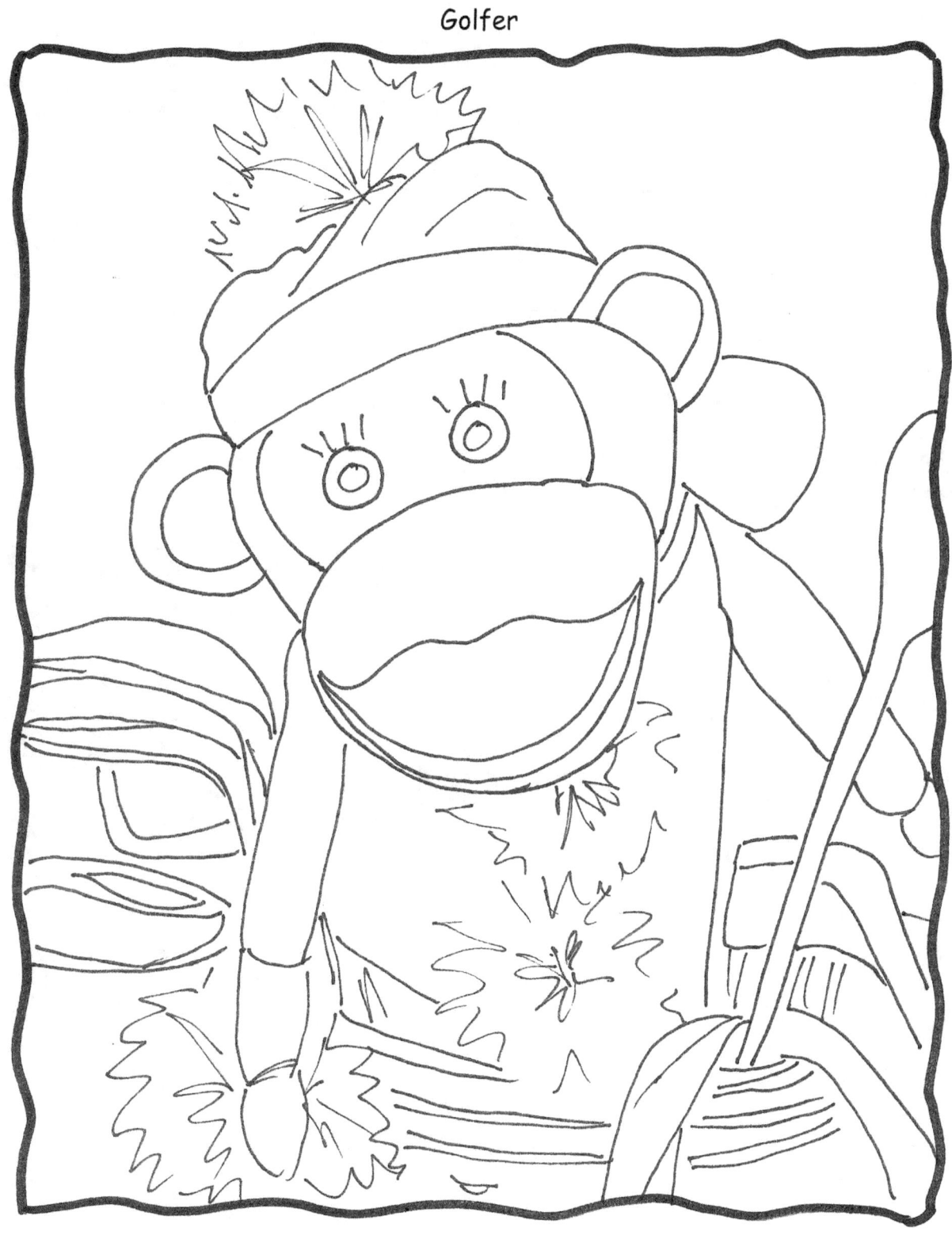

Mother and Child

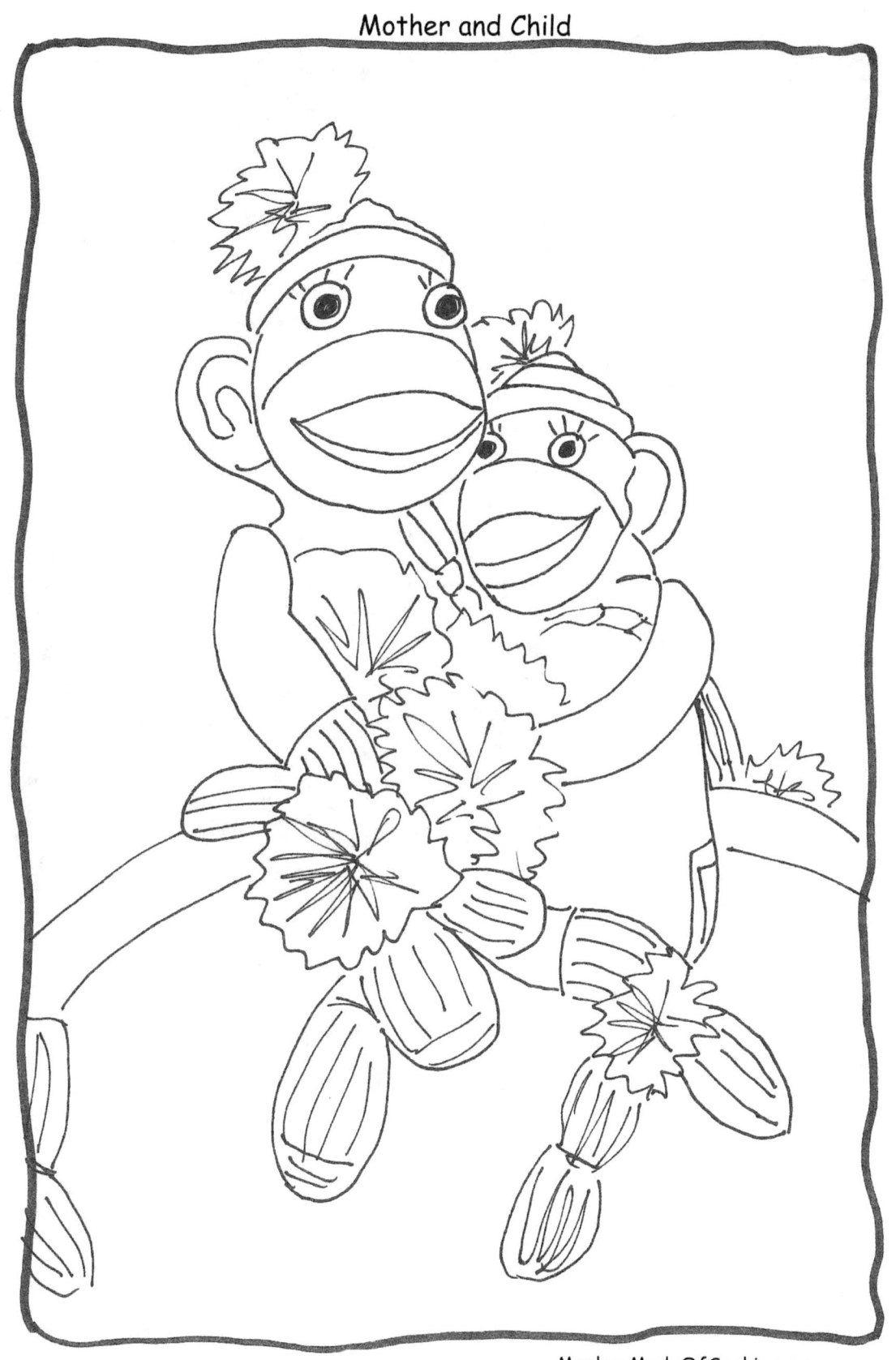

Mother's Day

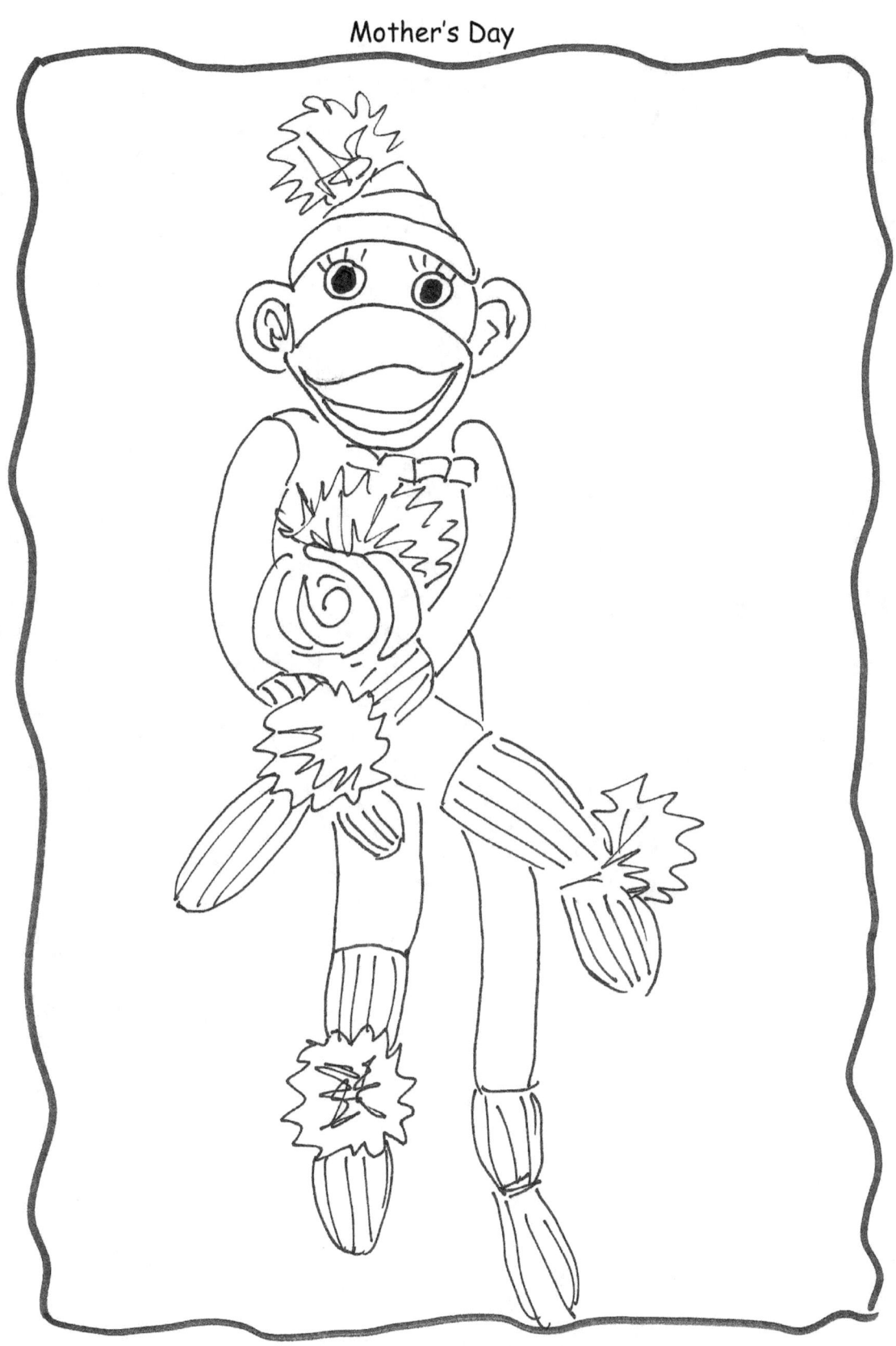

Night Night

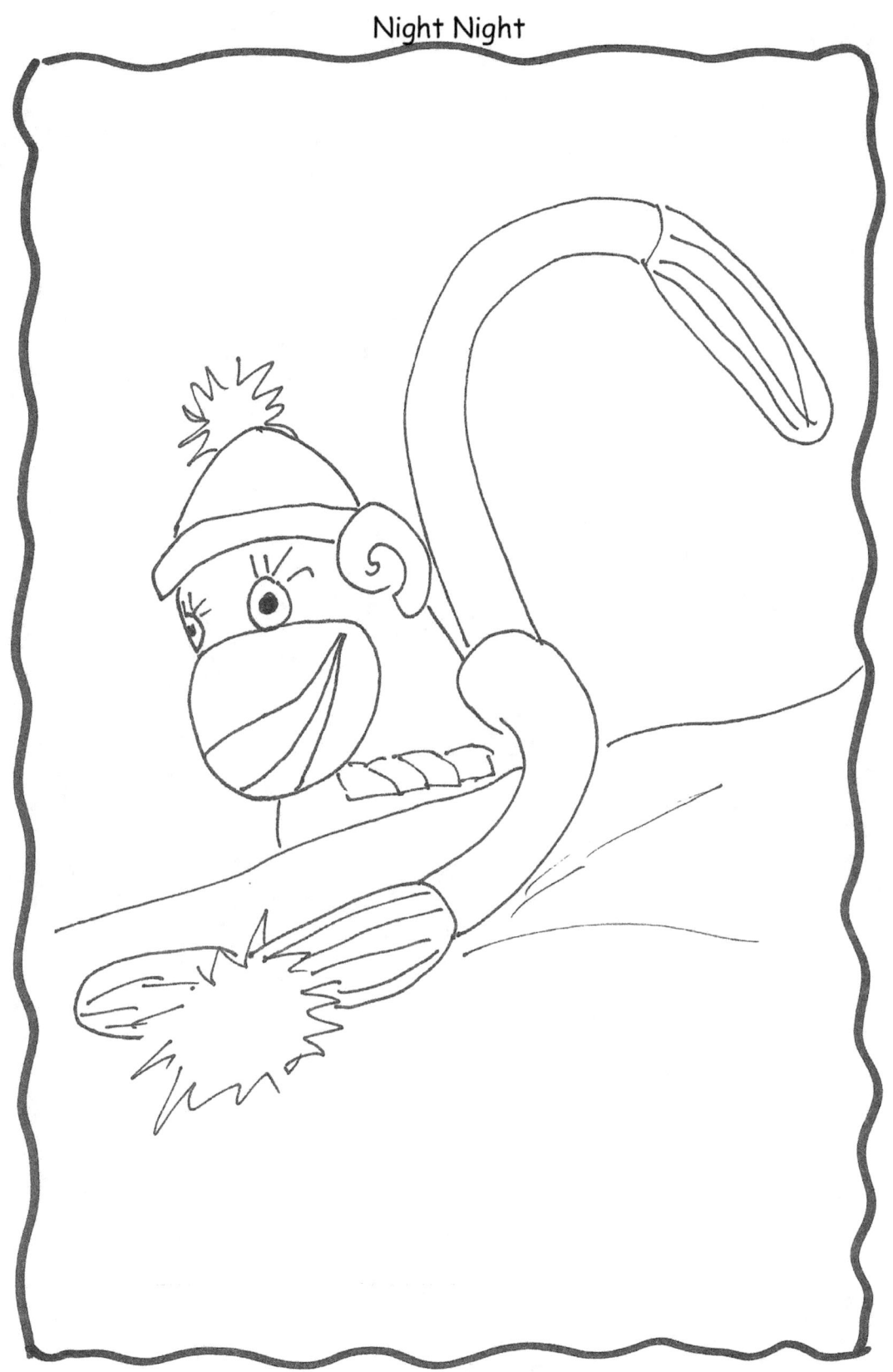

Hear No Bad Stuff

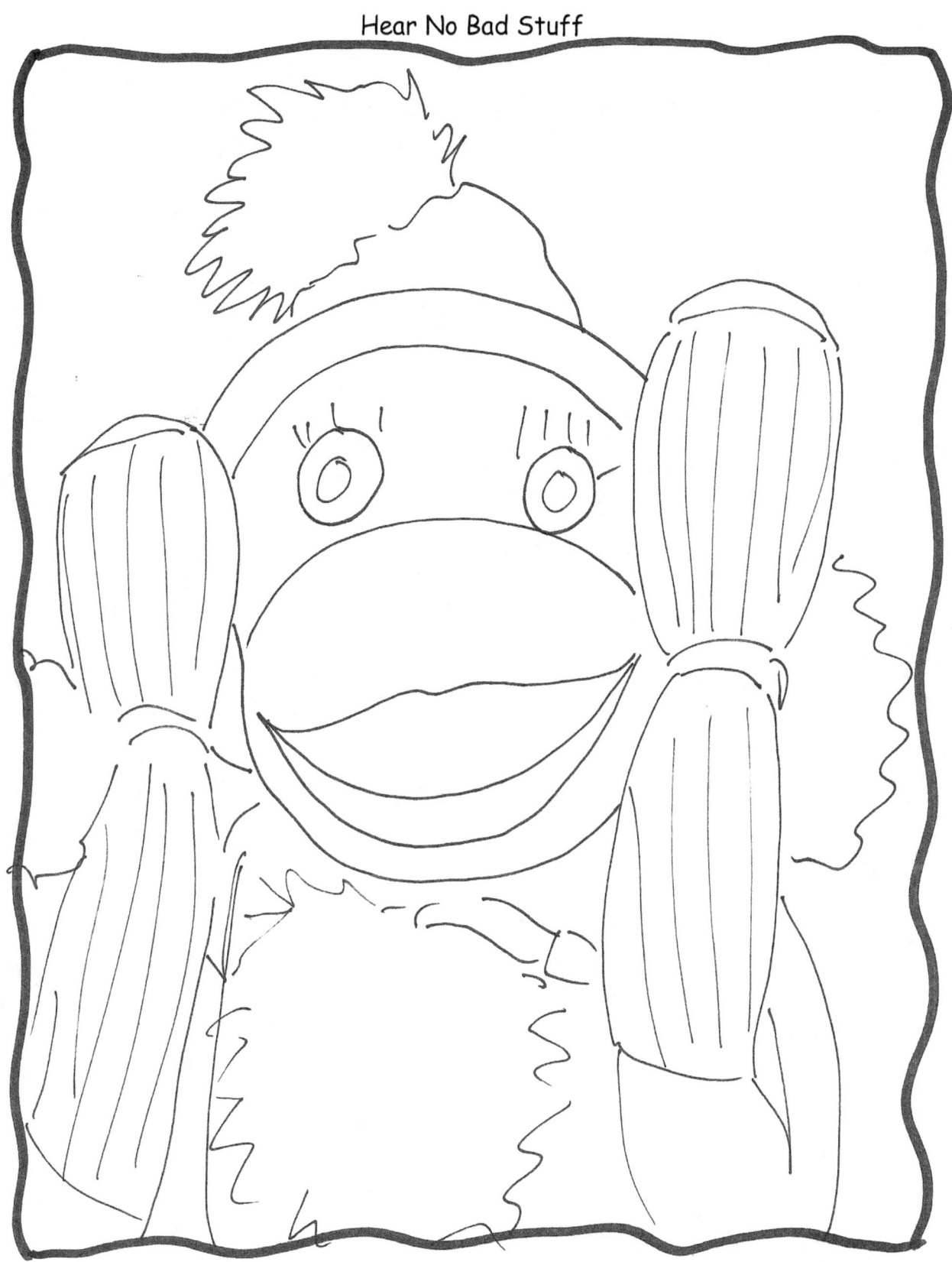

MonkeyMadeOfSockies.com

See No Bad Stuff

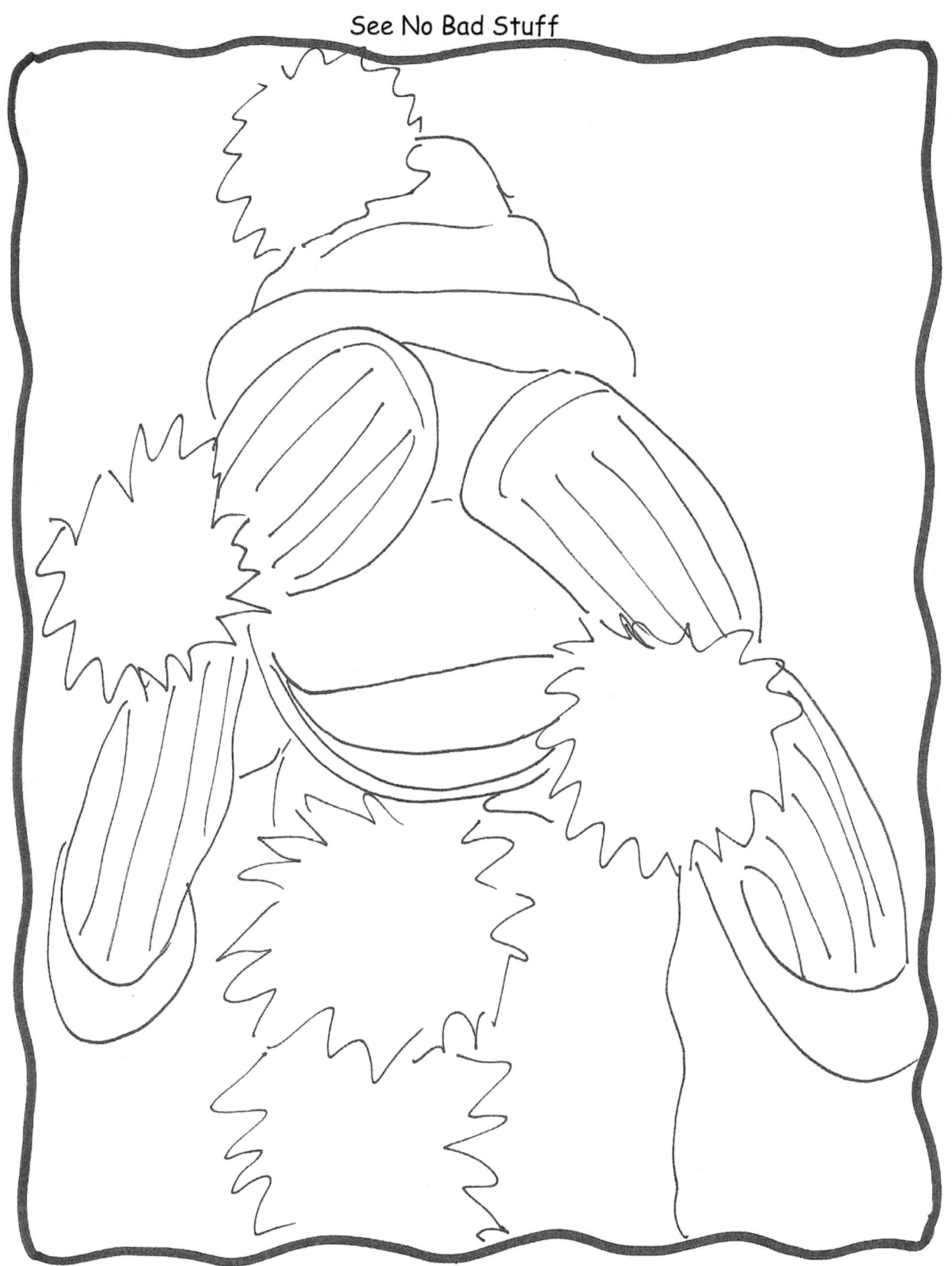

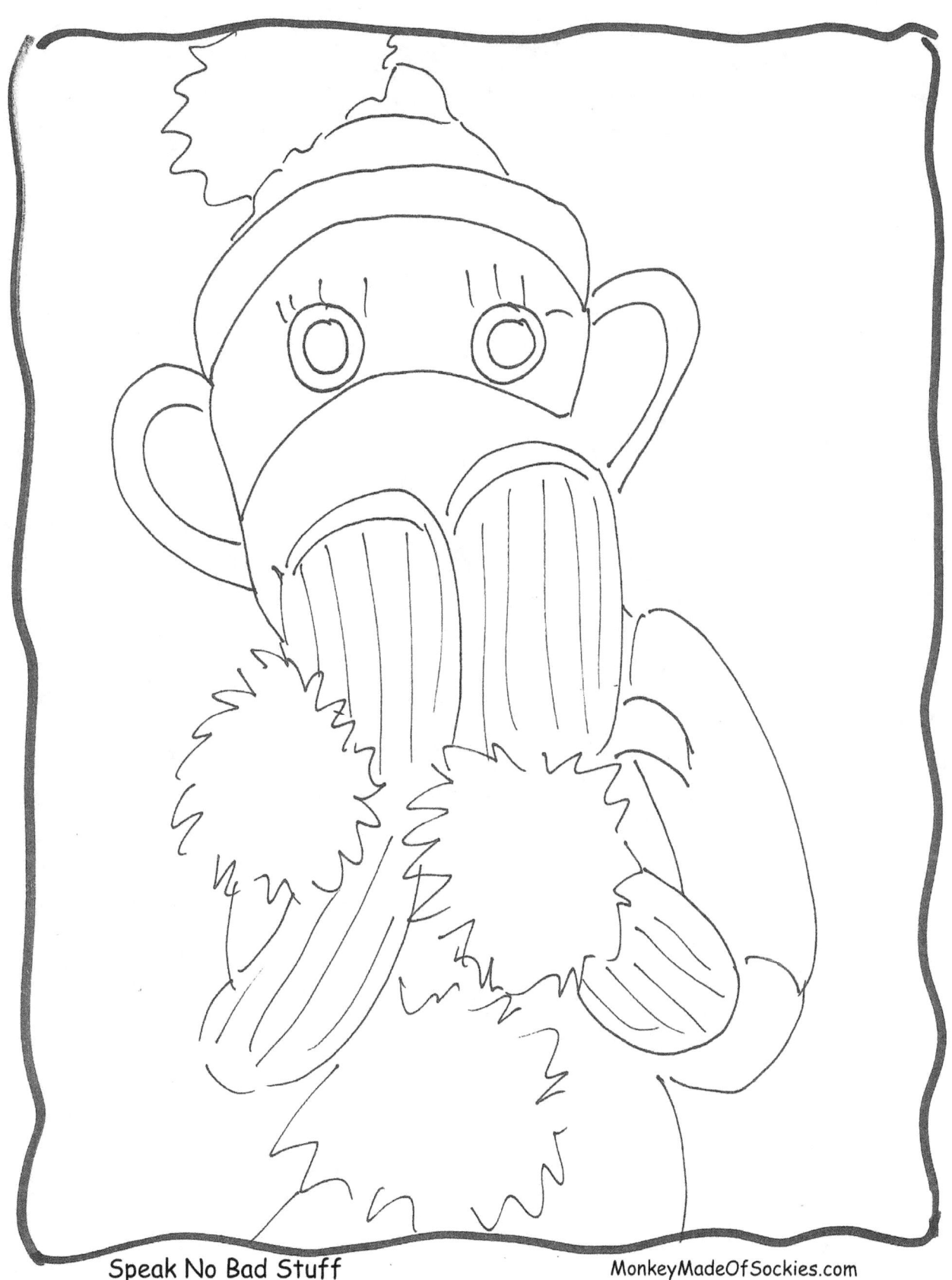

Speak No Bad Stuff

MonkeyMadeOfSockies.com

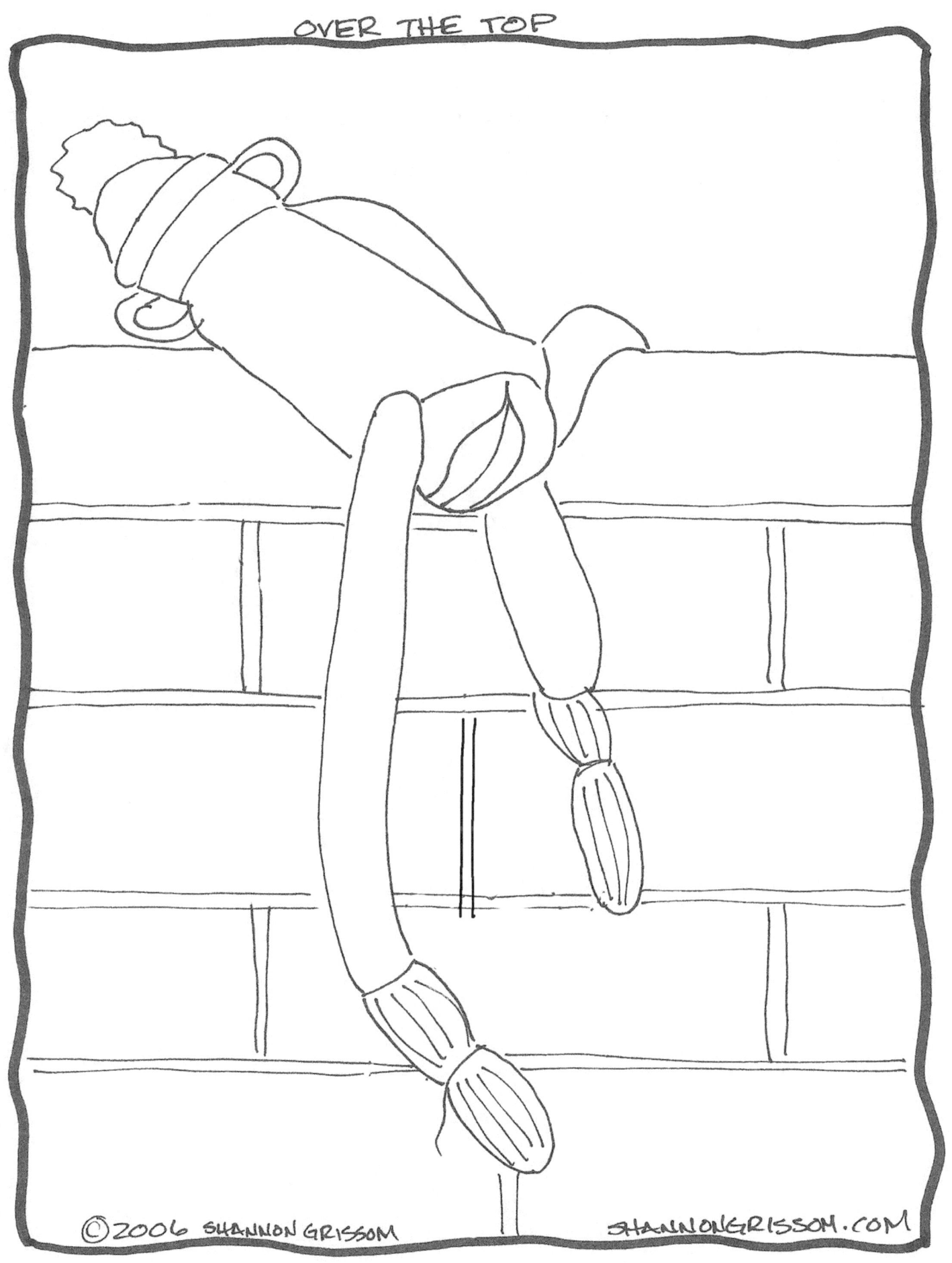

Patricia

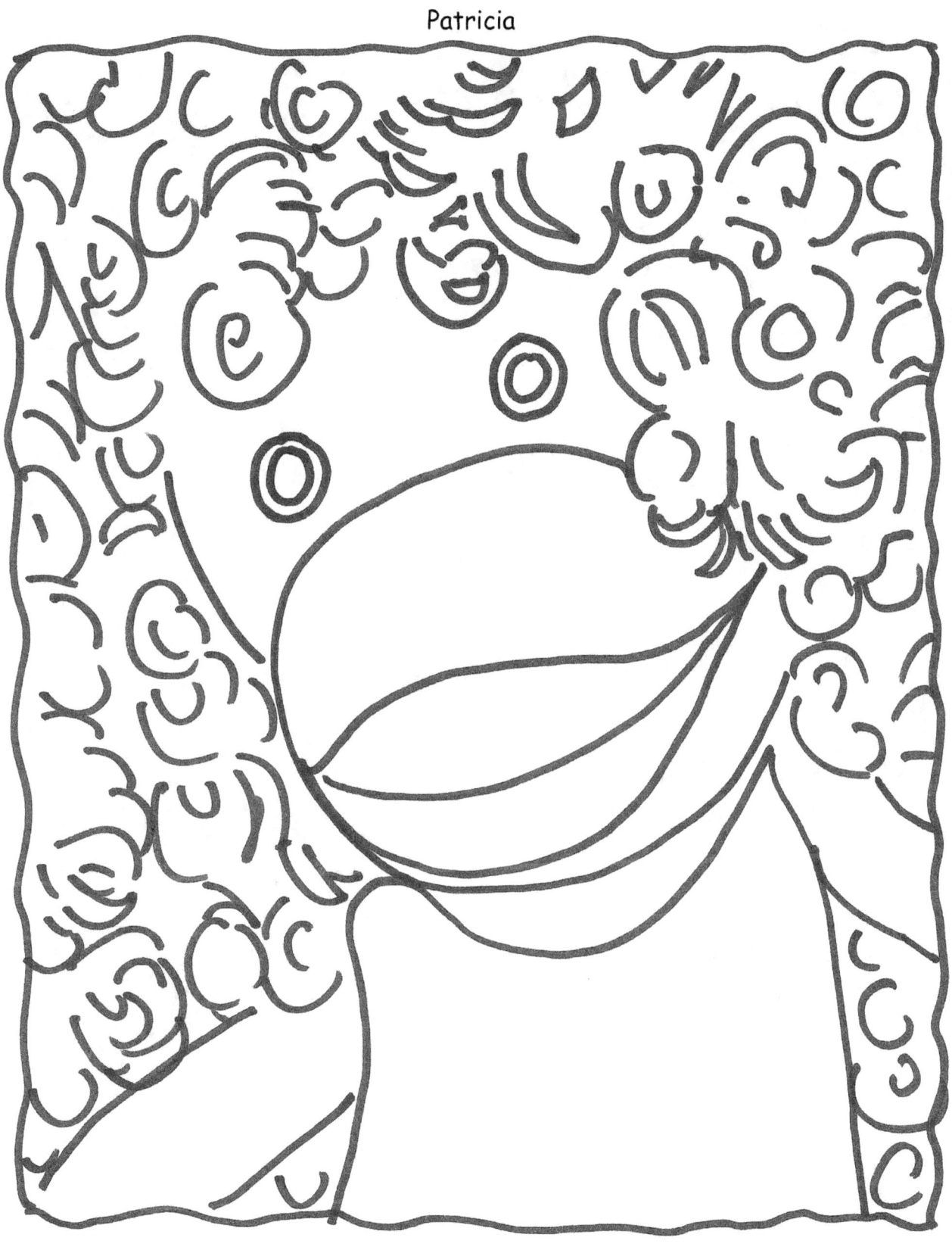

Pot ~ O' ~ Gold

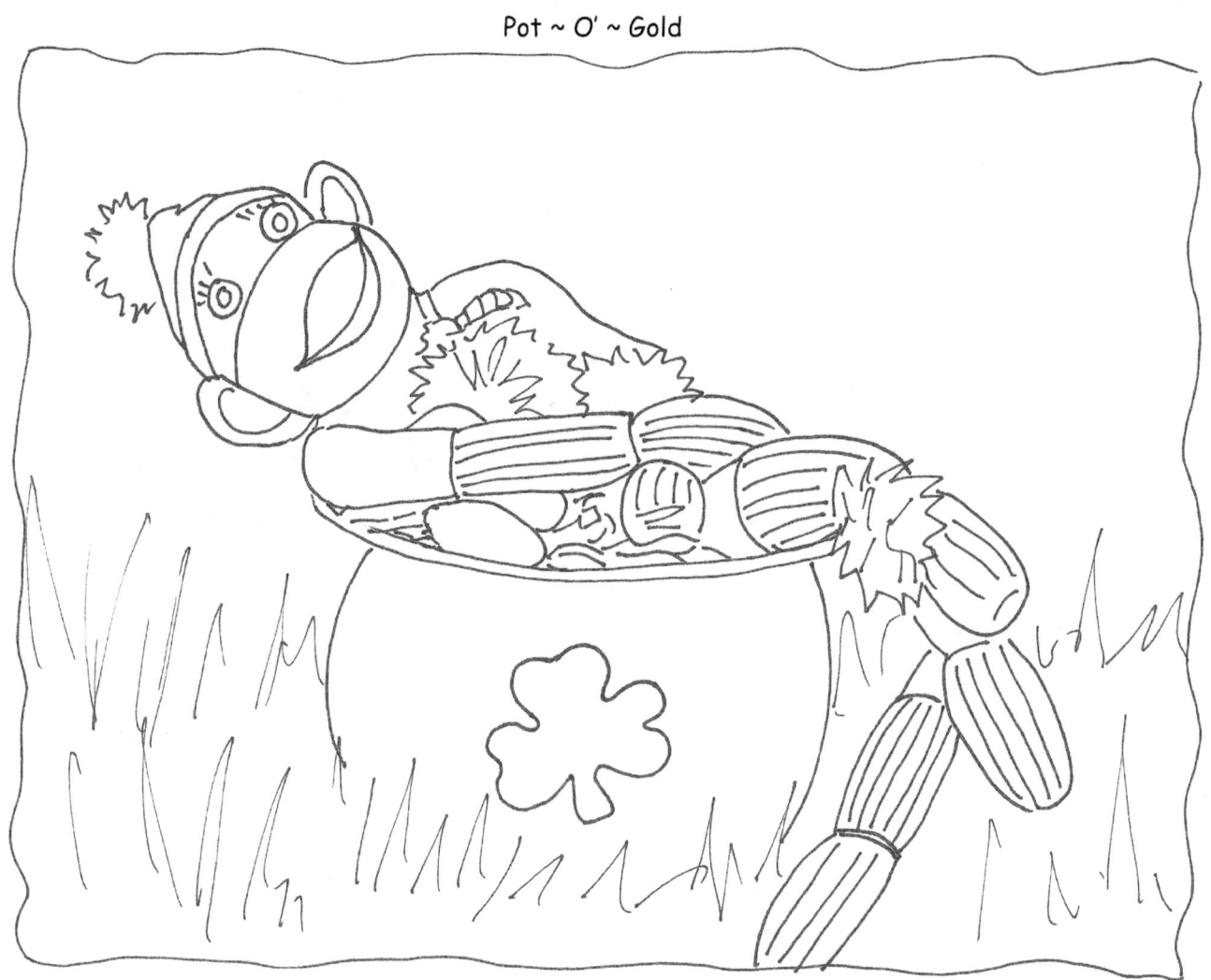

Pretzel

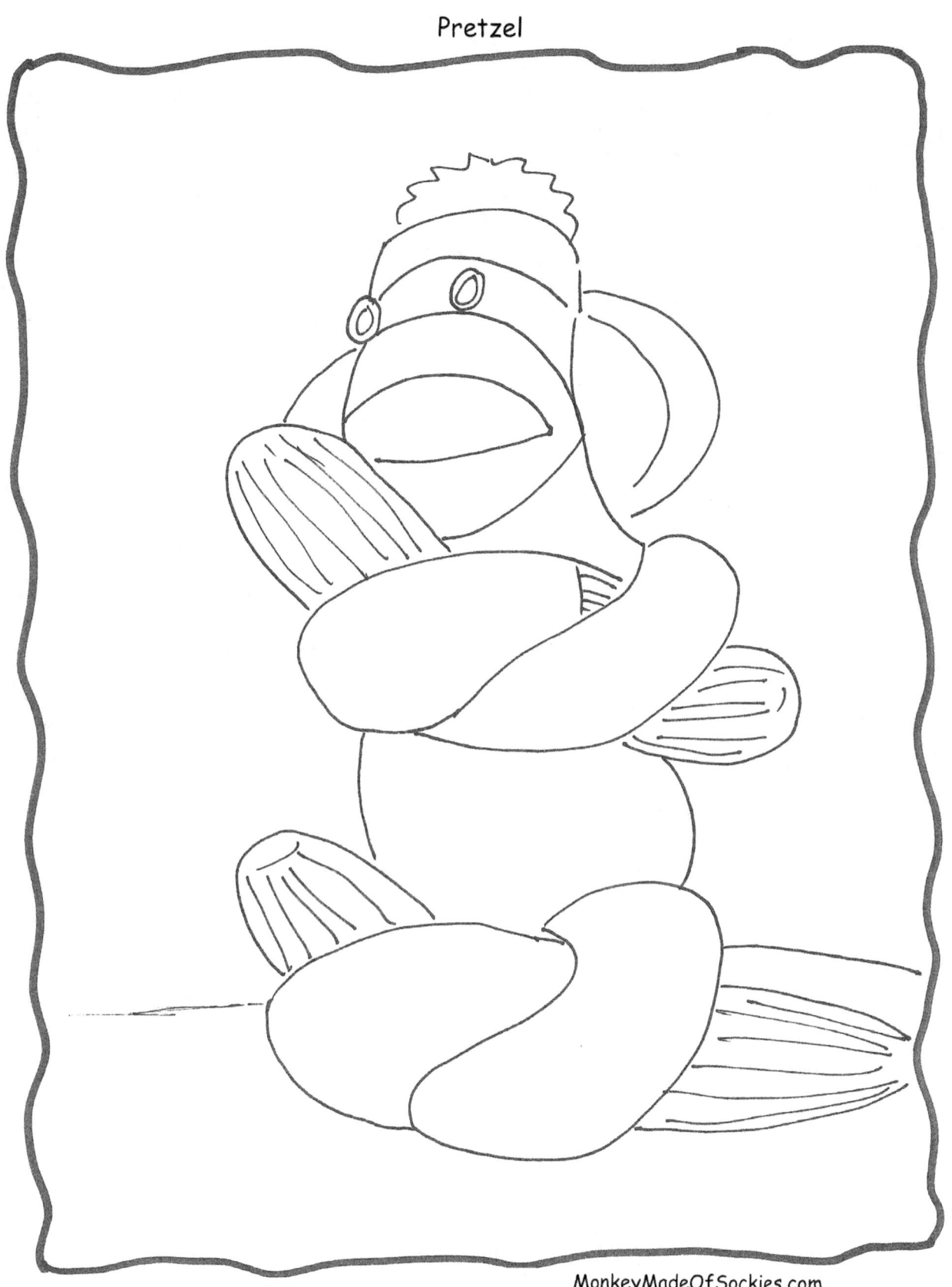

Profile

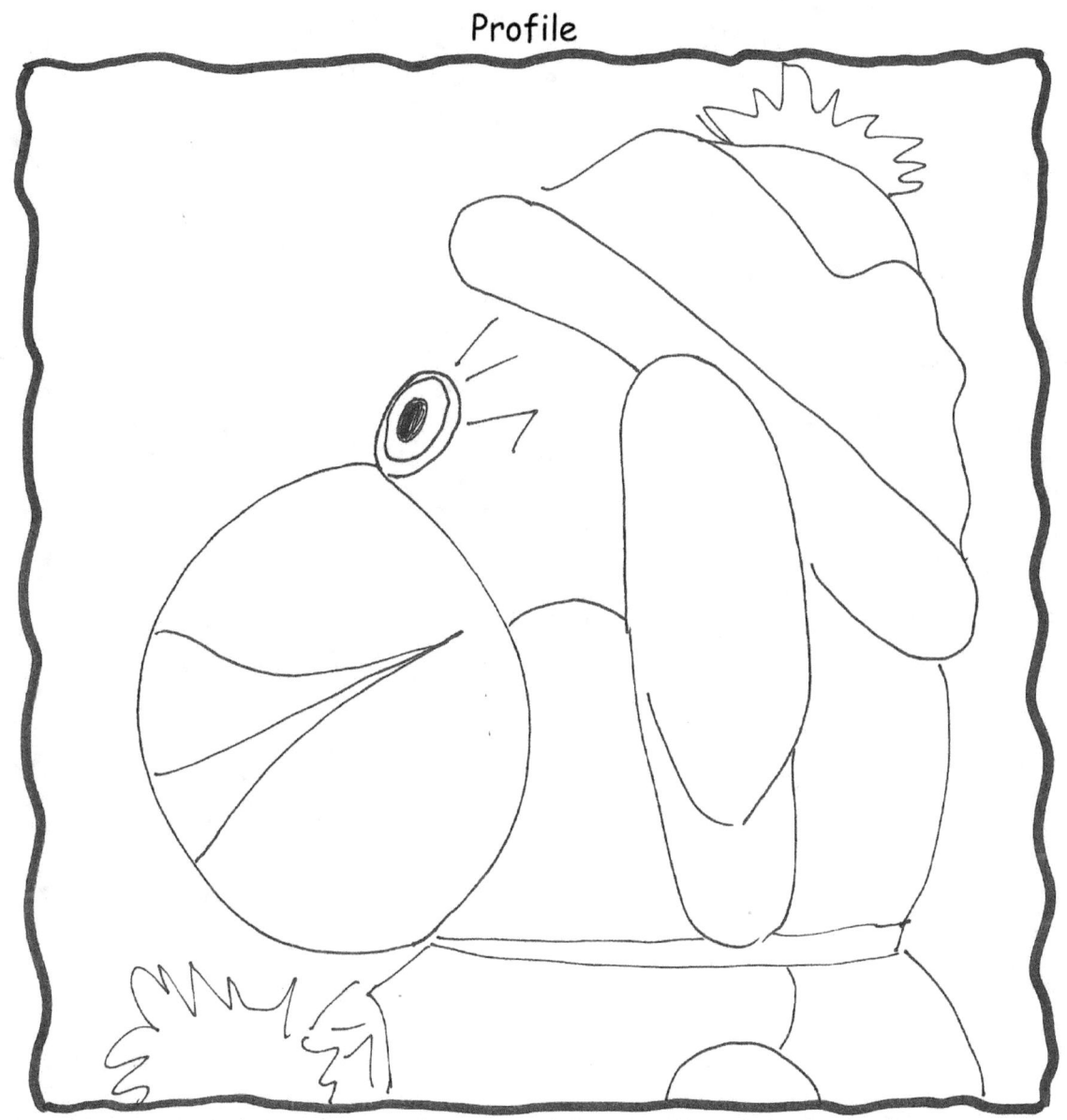

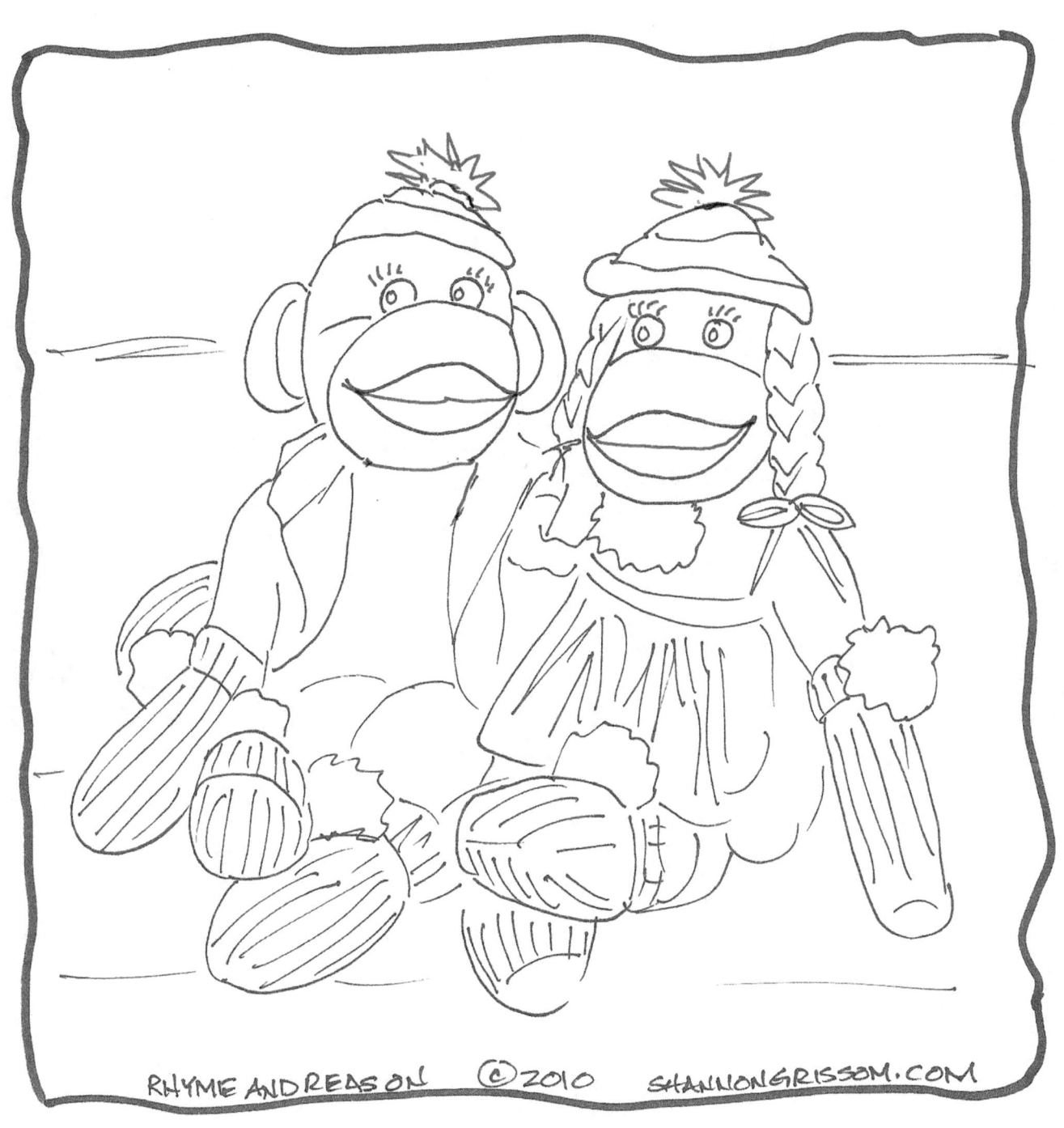

RHYME AND REASON   ©2010   SHANNONGRISSOM.COM

Stocking

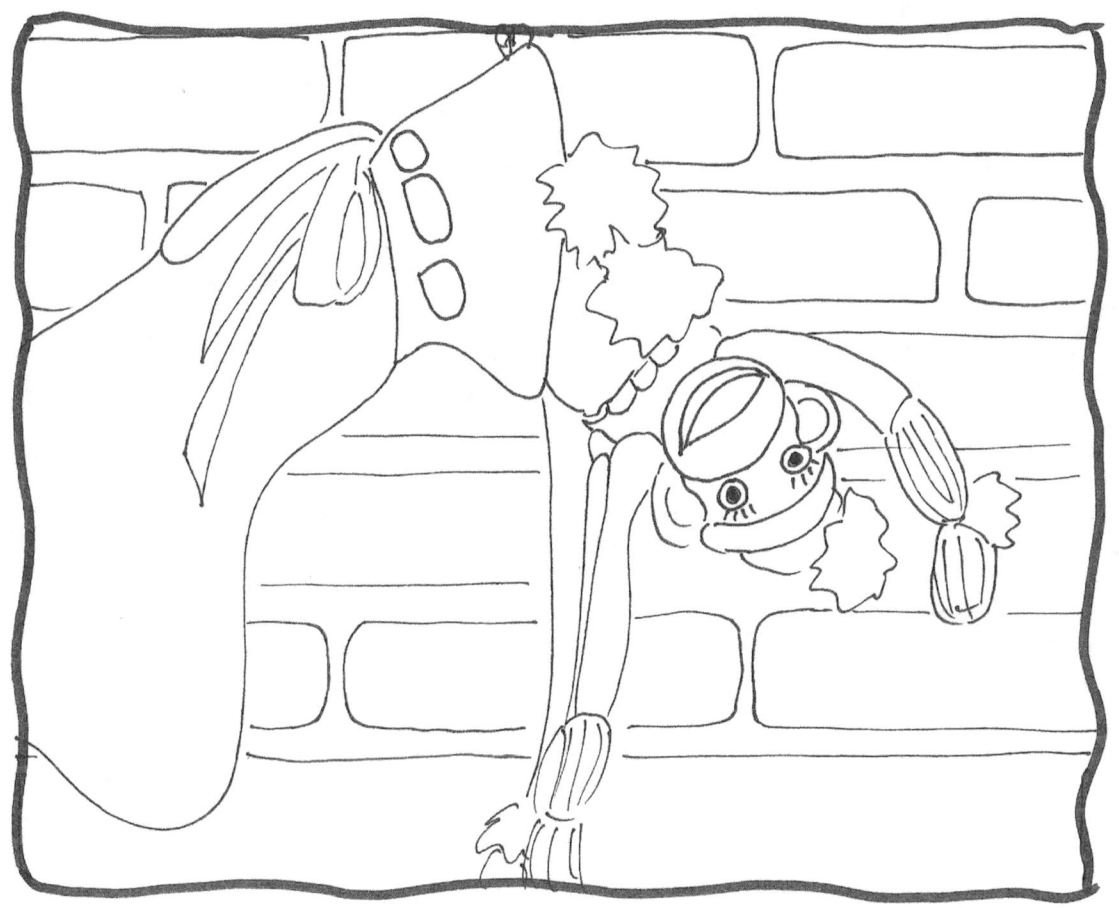

Sweetheart

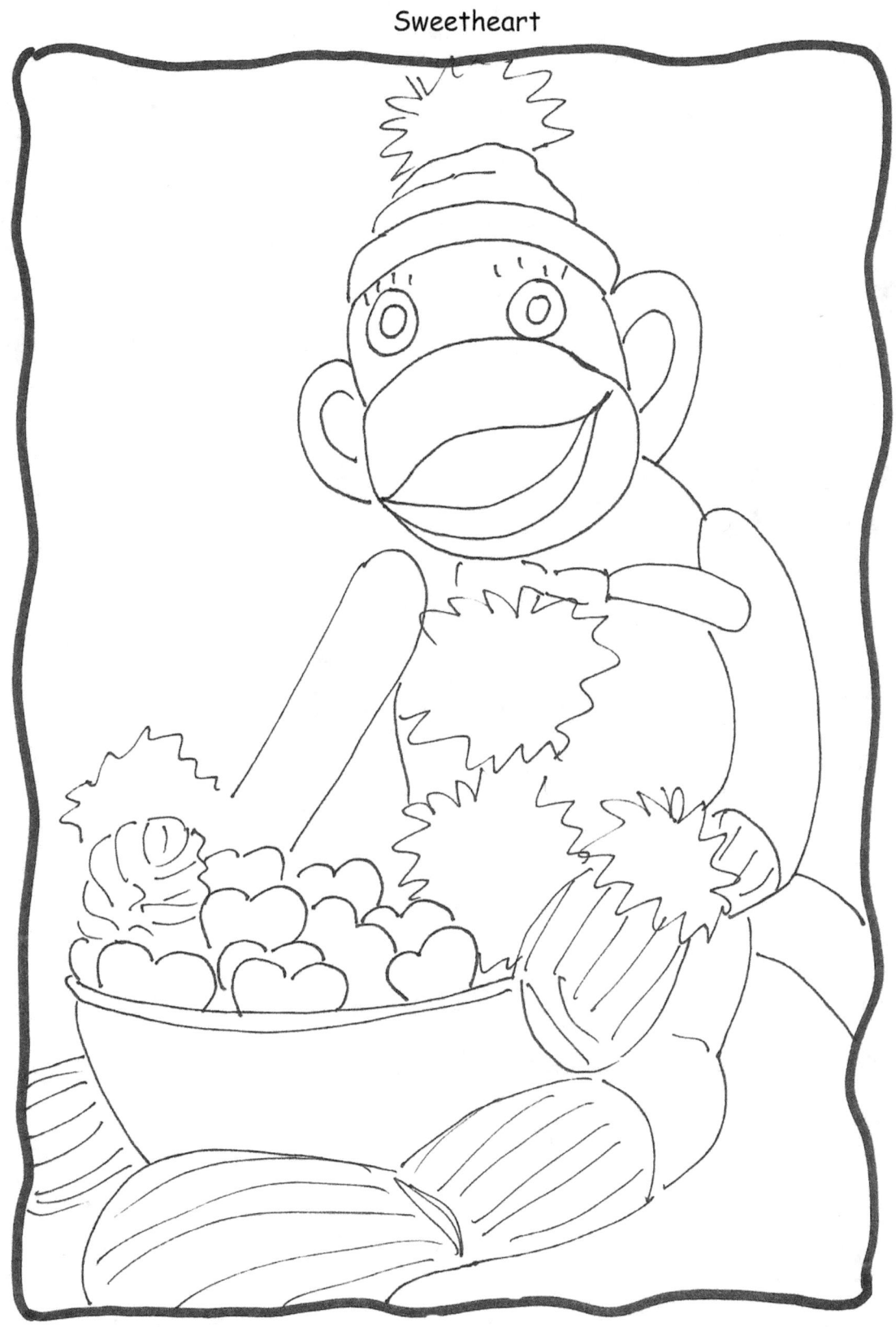

Touchdown!

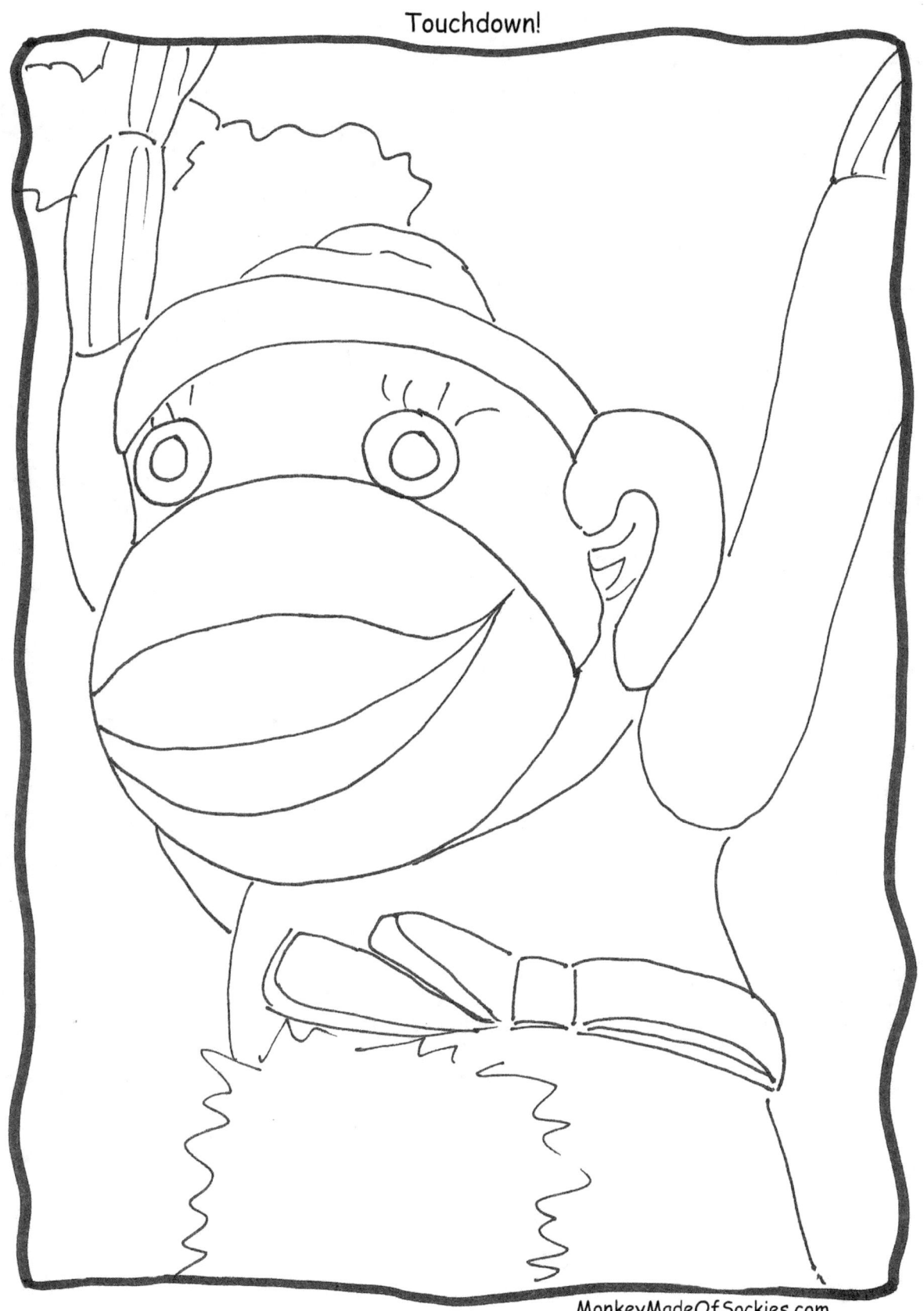

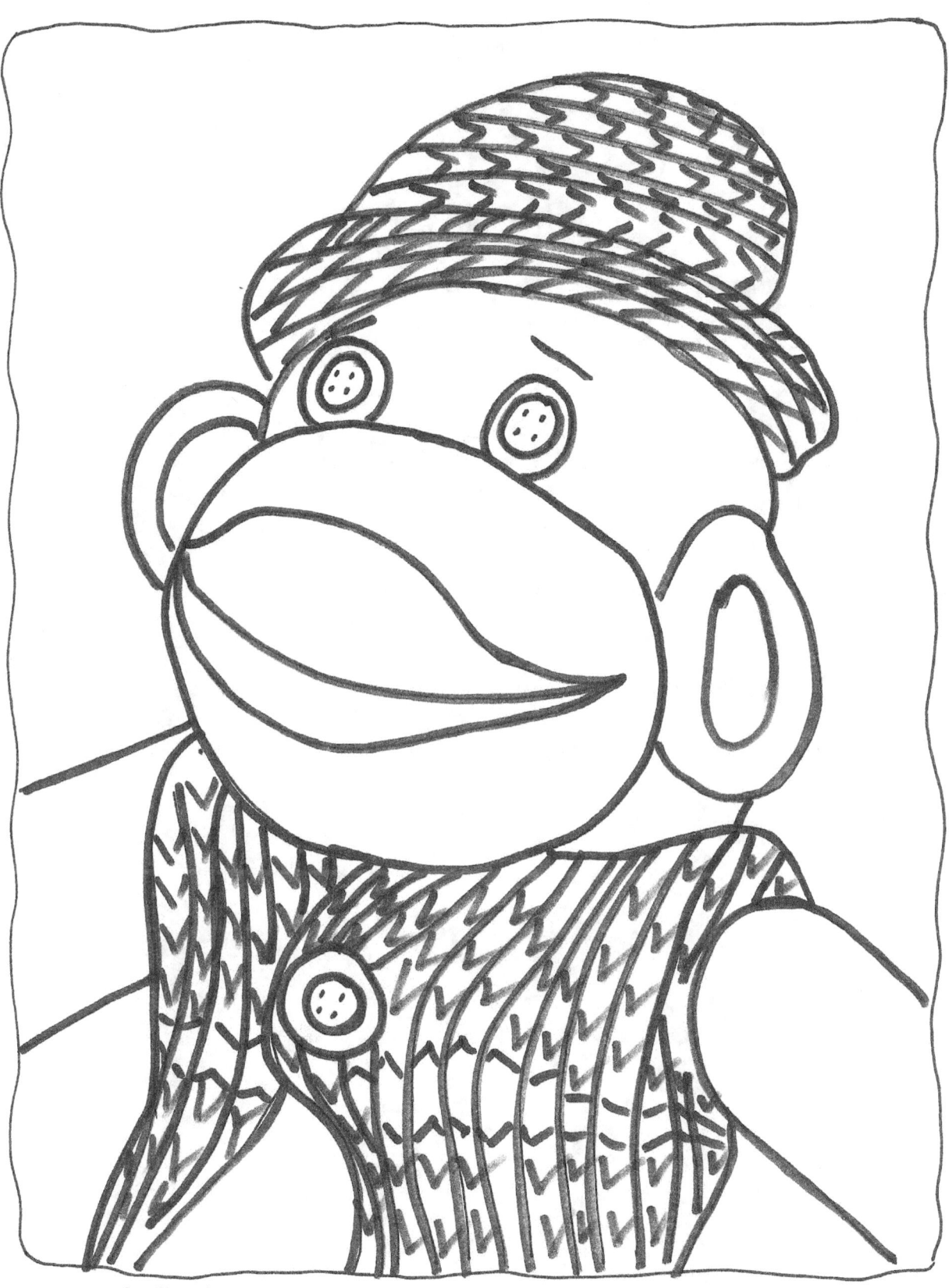

Uncle Frank

Valentine

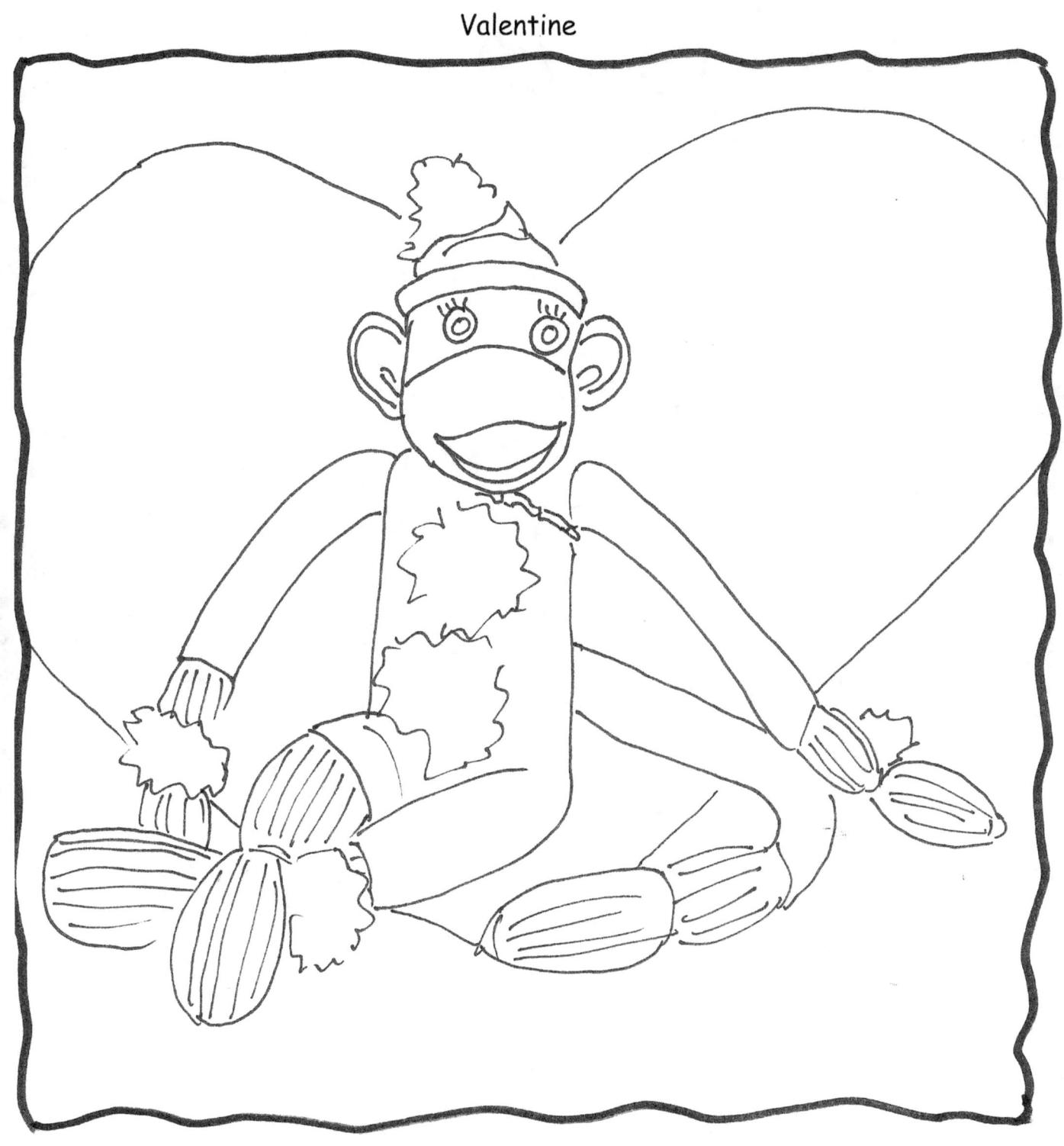

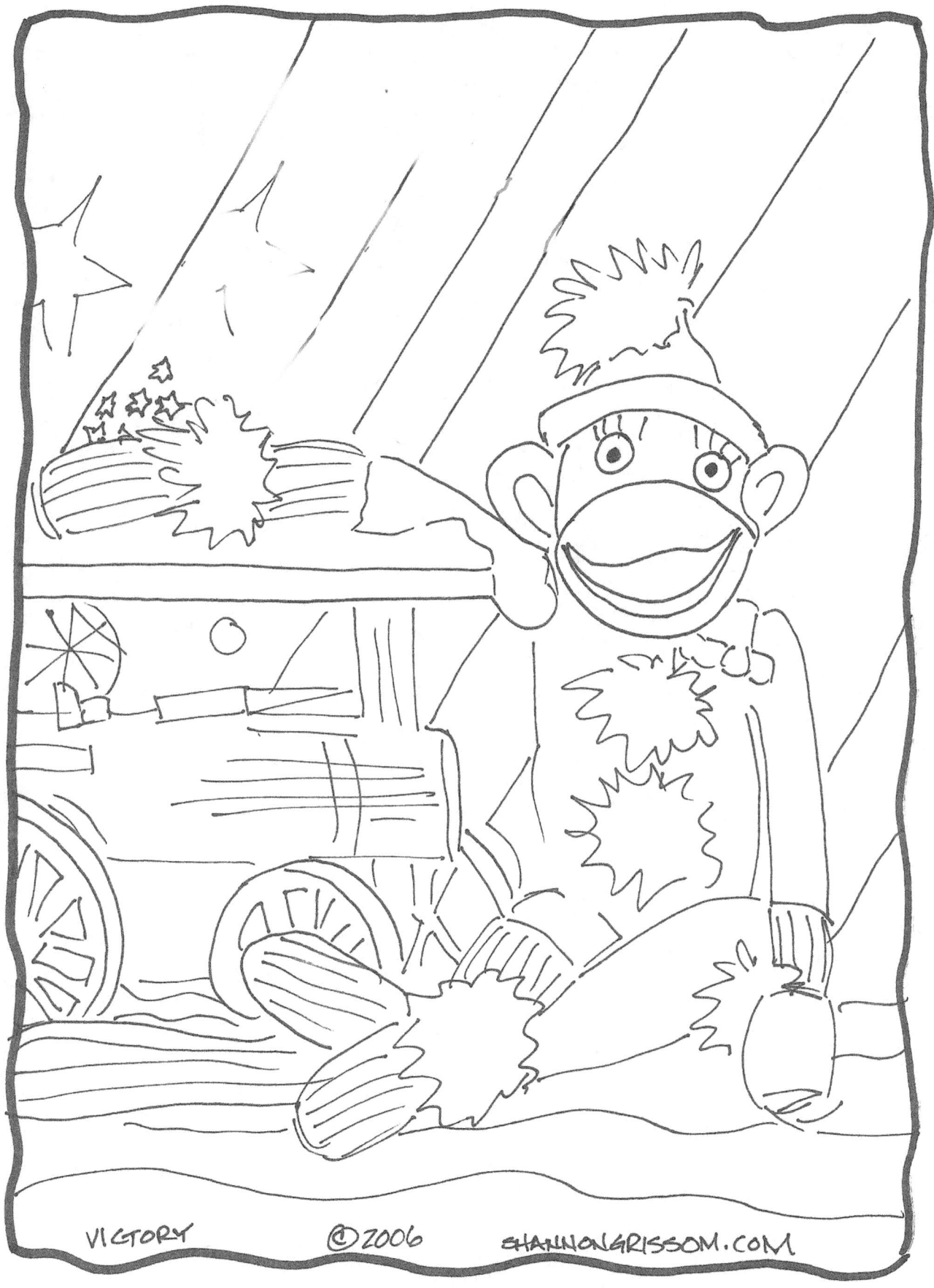

VICTORY ©2006 SHANNONGRISSOM.COM

Wanna Be A Rock N Roll Star

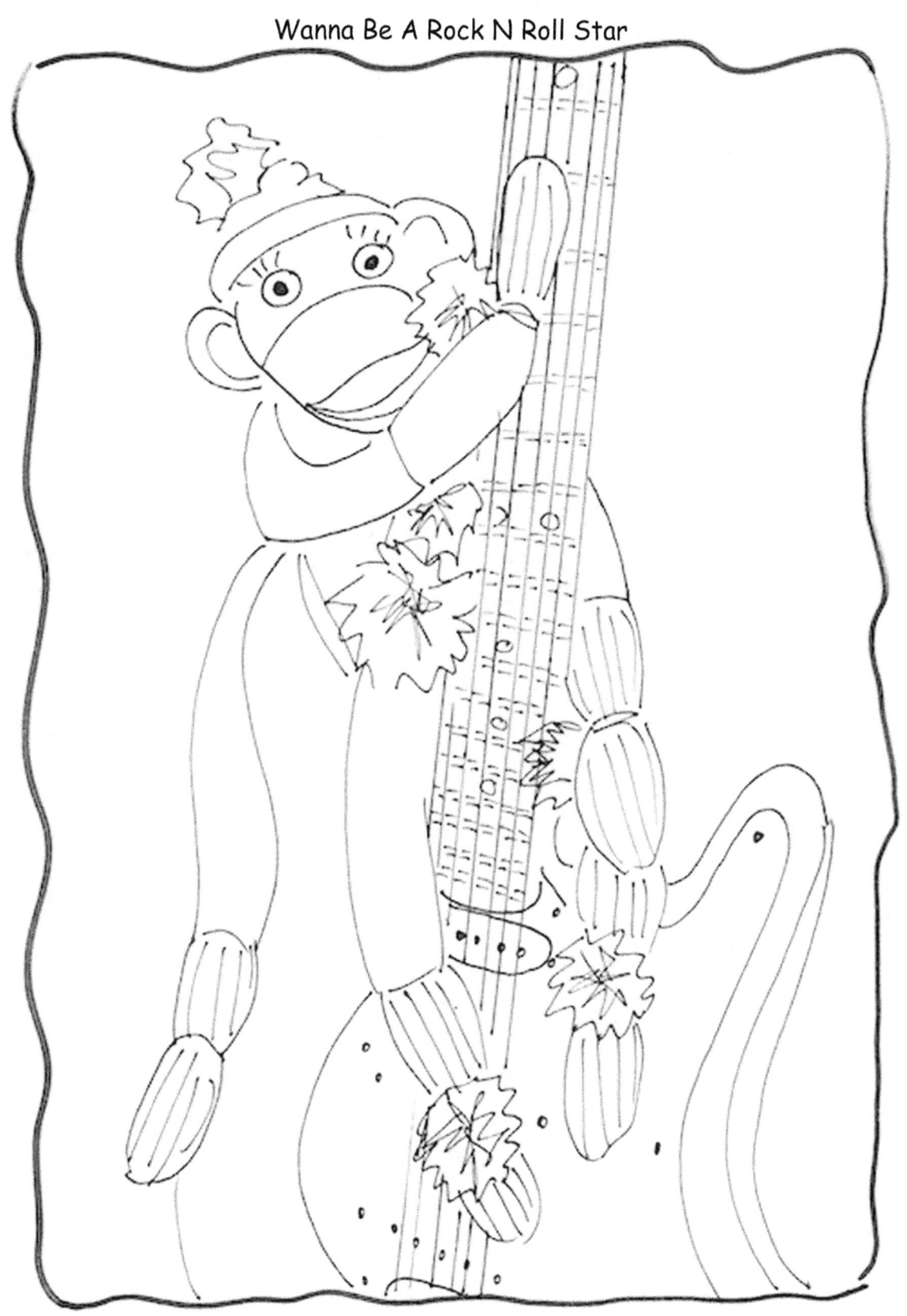

MonkeyMadeofSockies.com

Accordion

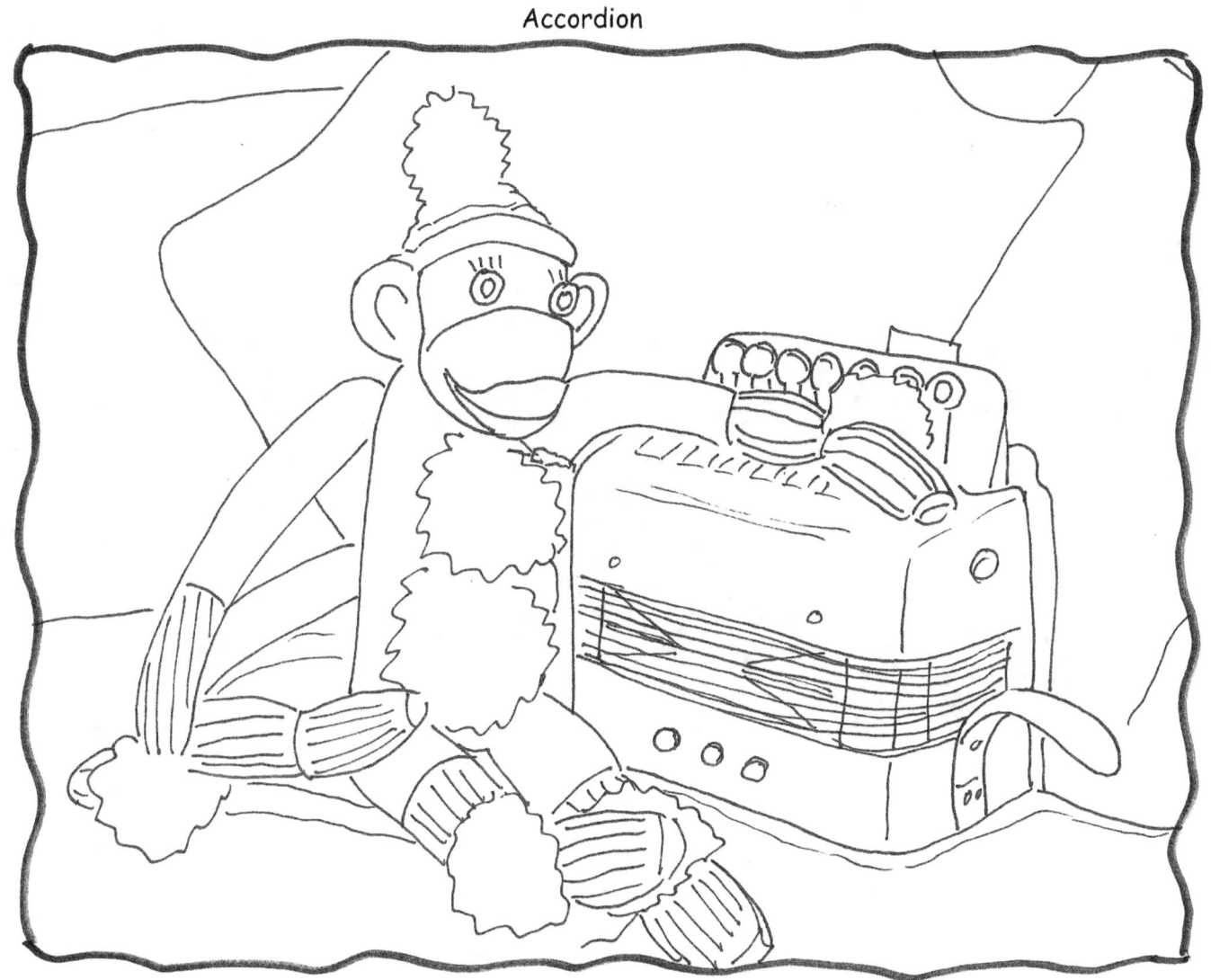

For More
Monkey Business
Visit

www.ShannonGrissom.com